Communications
in Computer and Information Science 1305

More information about this series at http://www.springer.com/series/7899

Ke Xu · Jianming Zhu ·
Xianhua Song · Zeguang Lu (Eds.)

Blockchain Technology and Application

Third CCF China Blockchain Conference, CBCC 2020
Jinan, China, December 18–20, 2020
Revised Selected Papers

 Springer

Editors
Ke Xu
Tsinghua University
Beijing, China

Xianhua Song
Harbin University of Science
and Technology
Harbin, China

Jianming Zhu
Central University of Finance
and Economics
Beijing, China

Zeguang Lu
National Academy of Guo Ding
Institute of Data Science
Beijing, China

ISSN 1865-0929   ISSN 1865-0937 (electronic)
Communications in Computer and Information Science
ISBN 978-981-33-6477-6   ISBN 978-981-33-6478-3 (eBook)
https://doi.org/10.1007/978-981-33-6478-3

This Springer imprint is published by the registered company Springer Nature Singapore Pte Ltd.
The registered company address is: 152 Beach Road, #21-01/04 Gateway East, Singapore 189721, Singapore

Preface

As the program chairs of the 2020 CCF China Blockchain Conference (CBCC 2020), it was our great pleasure to welcome you to the conference, which was held in Jinan, China, December 18–20, 2020, hosted by the China Computer Federation, the Blockchain Committee of the China Computer Federation, AnKe Blockchain Industrial Development Institute, Aisino Corporation, National Academy of Guo Ding Institute of Data Science, Shandong University, Dareway Software Co., Ltd., and Shandong Key Laboratory of Blockchain Finance. The goal of this conference was to provide a forum for blockchain scientists and engineers.

The conference attracted 64 paper submissions. After the hard work of the Program Committee, 8 papers were accepted to appear in the conference proceedings, with an acceptance rate of 12.5%. The major topic of this conference was blockchain science and technology.

We would like to thank all the Program Committee members (181 coming from 152 institutes) for their hard work in completing the review tasks. Their collective efforts made it possible to attain quality reviews for all the submissions within a few weeks. Their diverse expertise in each individual research area helped us to create an exciting program for the conference. Their comments and advice helped the authors to improve the quality of their papers and gain deeper insights.

Many thanks should also go to the authors and participants for their tremendous support in making the conference a success.

We thank Dr. Lanlan Chang and Jane Li from Springer, whose professional assistance was invaluable in the production of the proceedings.

Besides the technical program, CBCC 2020 offered different experiences to the participants and we hope that you enjoyed the conference.

November 2020

Ke Xu
Jianming Zhu

Organization

The 2020 CCF China Blockchain Conference (CBCC 2020), https://conf.ccf.org.cn/ CBCC2020, was held in Jinan, China, December 18–20, 2020, hosted by the China Computer Federation, the Blockchain Committee of the China Computer Federation, AnKe Blockchain Industrial Development Institute, Aisino Corporation, National Academy of Guo Ding Institute of Data Science, Shandong University, Dareway Software Co., Ltd., and Shandong Key Laboratory of Blockchain Finance.

Steering Committee Chairs

Chun Chen	Chinese Academy of Engineering, China
Zhongyi Zhou	Chinese Academy of Engineering, China
Chunming Rong	Norwegian Academy of Engineering, Norway

General Chairs

Xueming Si	Fudan University, China
Liehuang Zhu	Beijing Institute of Technology, China
Tianhui Ma	Aerospace Information Co., Ltd., China

Program Chairs

Ke Xu	Tsinghua University, China
Jianming Zhu	Central University of Finance and Economics, China

Organization Chairs

Yi Sun	Chinese Academy of Sciences, China
Lianhai Wang	Shandong Computer Science Center, China

Forum Chairs

Kai Lei	Peking University Shenzhen Graduate School, China
Hongzhang An	China Network Security Blockchain Research and Development, China

Publication Chairs

Liang Cai	Zhejiang University, China
Xianhua Song	Harbin University of Science and Technology, China
Zeguang Lu	National Academy of Guo Ding Institute of Data Science, China

Publicity Chairs

Wei Li	Hangzhou Qulian Technology Co., Ltd., China
Keke Gai	Beijing University of Technology, China

Contents

ChainSim: A P2P Blockchain Simulation Framework

Bozhi Wang[1,2(✉)], Shiping Chen[1,2], Lina Yao[1], and Qin Wang[2,3]

[1] University of New South Wales, Sydney, NSW 2062, Australia
bozhi.wang@student.unsw.edu.au
[2] CSIRO Data61, Sydney, NSW 2110, Australia
[3] Swinburne University of Technology, Melbourne, VIC 3122, Australia

Abstract. In the past few years, blockchains have been one of the most attractive emerging technologies. Many researchers and institutions have devoted their resources to the development of more effective blockchain technologies and innovative applications. However, with the limitation of computing power and financial resources, it is hard for researchers to deploy and test their blockchain innovations in a large-scape physical network. In this paper, we design a peer to peer blockchain simulation framework to address this challenge, called ChainSim. ChainSim provides a foundation and skeleton to argument and simulate as large as thousand-nodes P2P blockchain network with a single computer. This paper presents ChainSim basic structure and simulation mechanism; and showcase ChainSim capabilities and usefulness. With ChainSim, researchers can test their new consensus protocols, reproduce a subtle security attack and evaluate its risks with a large number of nodes under heavily transaction loads.

Keywords: Blockchain · Peer to peer · Simulation

1 Introduction

Since 2008, Satoshi Nakamoto published the Bitcoin whitepaper online [1], Blockchain has shown its potentials in many areas. From cryptocurrency to cross-border payment, distributed storage, supply chain management, more and more applications are going to set blockchain as a fundamental technology. To meet the needs of the development of these applications, several decentralized applications (Dapps) platforms has been published, such as Ethereum [2] and Fabric [3]. In Ethereum, anyone can "upload" Dapps to Ethereum and they will always run as programmed. This enables people to develop varieties of financial applications which are decentralized, without any single organization or person controlling them. The running program needs a native cryptocurrency called Ether (ETH) which is mined similar with Bitcoin. The consensus mechanism used in Ethereum is proof of work (PoW), which will be changed to proof of stake (PoS) in the coming future. Fabric is the other famous Dapp platform which provides a modular and extendable architecture. Fabric supports digital certificate identity authentication form, which is anonymous authentication in Ethereum. There is no general token like ETH

© Springer Nature Singapore Pte Ltd. 2021
K. Xu et al. (Eds.): CBCC 2020, CCIS 1305, pp. 1–16, 2021.
https://doi.org/10.1007/978-981-33-6478-3_1

in Fabric, it is mostly focus on federated blockchain used within a group of semi-trust organizations. The consensus of Fabric is multiple, in most cases based on Practical Byzantine Fault Tolerance (PBFT).

However, there are still blanks between development and deployment of new consensus protocols and new applications. As the mining part of blockchain needs a lot of power, the cost of blockchain usage keeps in a high level. That also hinder the research and development of blockchain. Researchers need have enough money or computing power to set up a private chain or deploy on the real chain to test their new ideas. However, all blockchains are distributed, cannot be controlled by a single person, and also hard to change. It is difficult for researchers to change key parameters of main chain and observe the effects of changes. Also, it is nearly impossible to reproduce some special issues in a real blockchain, such as transaction attack, network attack and other vulnerability attack.

In this paper, we propose ChainSim, a P2P blockchain simulator framework, to address the above challenges. The key idea is to use light weight threads to simulate a large P2P blockchain in a single desktop/laptop computer. With ChainSim, we can change the key parameters such as miner number, mining difficulty, block size, etc. Since our simulator is time sequence and event-driven simulation, we can observe and record the response of any input during any time or any stage of simulation. At the same time, our simulator is modularized. We can change the working mode of the simulator to meet different needs. The communication mode between nodes can be chosen as broadcast, multicast, gossip or other types. The simulator also can be switched to different consensus mechanisms, no matter PoW, POS, PBFT or Tangle [4].

The rest of this paper is organized as follows. Section 2 shows the structure and functions of this P2P blockchain simulation framework. In Sect. 3 we deploy three different types of blockchain demos: Bitcoin, Ethereum and IOTA in our ChainSim framework. Section 4 presents some related work. We conclude the paper in Sect. 5.

2   ChainSim: Design Principles

The blockchain is essentially a distributed ledger database over a peer-to-peer network. Unlike storing all ledgers in a centralized server or cluster, the distributed structure of the blockchain allows all nodes in the network to store all data in the chain synchronously. At the same time, the generation of distributed data blocks are subject to a specific consensus algorithm and protocol executed on each peer node. These blocks form a cryptographic account book which is under time sequence and hard to be changed. Through the blockchain technology, any network users who do not know each other can rely on the data on the blockchain to do business without any centralized trustworthy institutions.

In order to simulate the entire blockchain network on a single personal computer, we divide the basic structure of the blockchain into three layers: network layer, data layer and application layer, as shown in Fig. 1. The network layer mainly implements the information transmission and network delay in P2P network. The data layer, which means miner layer, mainly contains the public ledger, consensus algorithm and corresponding blockchain protocol. The application layer, which always equals the user layer, mainly focuses on the transaction generation and business logic such as smart contracts. In order to save computing power and speed up the simulation time, we removed the encryption and decryption processes (including hash operations) of transactions and blocks in the simulation demos mentioned in this article, and replaced all this kind of operation with a random time-passing in a certain range. In subsequent use, this delay can be reverted to cryptographic operations as needed.

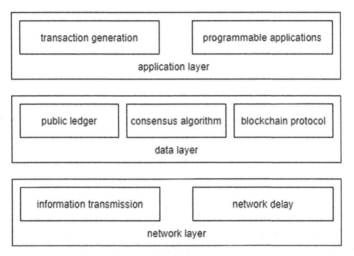

Fig. 1. ChainSim structure

The order of transaction propagation is shown in Fig. 2. After the user node generates a new transaction, it sends a transaction containing the necessary information to the network module. The network module adds a delay to it and sends it to the miner node. After receiving a transaction, the miner node puts it into the mempool. At the same time, the miner node competes the right of accounting the new block. When winning, package the transactions as a block and send the block to the network module. The network module sends the block to the miner nodes/all nodes according to the set transmission method. After receiving the block, the miner node processes it according to the consensus algorithm or blockchain protocol.

Next, we will introduce the three layers of ChainSim according to the consensus process of transaction.

2.1 Application Layer

The application layer is located in the first step of the entire transaction consensus process. The user node is the module with the largest number and the simplest function in the our simulation system. Its main functions include generating transactions, sending transactions, and receiving transaction completion progress information. Each user node maintains a local ledger, which contains historically completed transactions and transactions that have not been confirmed in the blockchain.

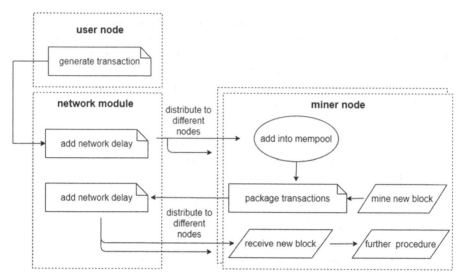

Fig. 2. Transaction propagation flow in normal blockchain network

In our simulation, the user node will continuously send transactions to the network module at a random time interval, which can be configured as a simulation argument. After the user node sends a transaction, the node's procedure will be in sleep mode until the historical transaction confirmation message is received or the next transaction is ready to be sent. Under our simulation framework, the system supports more than 30,000 nodes working at the same time with an ordinary laptop (hardware/software) configuration, which will be specified late in the paper.

Transaction is the most basic unit of information in the entire simulation system. A simple transaction usually includes: timestamp, user ID, transaction ID, sending mode, message size, specific transaction information. The sending mode is usually broadcast to all miner nodes. The specific transaction information is usually related to the blockchain protocol. For example, in the Bitcoin demo, the specific transaction information includes: timestamp, sender ID, receiver ID, token number, and other text information. In the Ethereum demo, we have further expanded the text information so that it can send smart contracts or call smart contracts. We will mention the specific content in Sect. 3.

In a blockchain system with currency, we usually hang the tokens in a sent but unconfirmed transaction. It cannot be used again before receiving the confirmation message, but the node can still send a new transaction without the usage of these hanging tokens. In contrast, we can set some user nodes not to hang these tokens, to test the impact of the double spending attack.

2.2 Network Layer

In order to achieve different transmission methods and network delays more efficiently, we transfer all the messages in the system that needs to be transmitted through the network, whether it is an independent transaction, a block or a request, through a network module. The transmission method may be unicast, broadcast, multicast, or gossip.

When the network module receives a message, it will split a single message containing N target nodes into N single message each message will be sent to a single node. Then determine the network delay of this transmission by the transmission method and the distance between sending node and target node. This delay value will be added to the message and sent to the information receiving module of the target node.

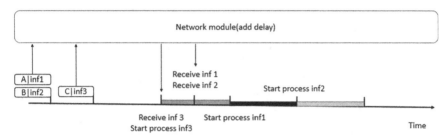

Fig. 3. Network delay

As shown in Fig. 3, when the node's information receiving module receives a new message, it will determine the specific time that the node receives the message header according to the timestamp and delay time in the message, and insert it into the waiting queue in chronological order. When the receiving module is idle, it starts to receive the latest message in the waiting queue, and calculates the transmission delay according to the current node's transmission speed and message size, then keep the receiving module busy during this time.

2.3 Data Layer

The work of the data layer is mainly completed by the miner nodes. The miner node is the part with the largest workload and the most complicated work content in the entire simulation framework. It mainly includes an information receiving module, an information processing module and a consensus module (Fig. 4).

As mentioned in Subsect. 2.2, the information receiving module arranges the external information in time sequence, and confirms whether this message is received completely and enters the storage space of this node at the current moment.

The information processing module will further process the message, such as transaction, block or other message, in the storage space. For example, in Bitcoin case, a new transaction will be placed in mempool. A new block will be verified. If valid, the block will be written to the node's chain, switch the state of the block before 6 blocks to be confirmed, and send a stop command to the consensus module to stop current mining. The work of the consensus module is mainly based on different blockchain protocols. For example, in Bitcoin case, the consensus module will follow the most recent block to mine the new block. We use a random mining time to represent the hash operation, keeping the consensus module busy during this mining time. If at the end of the mining time, the stop command sending by the information processing module has not received, it is deemed that the miner node has successfully mined a new block. The node will package

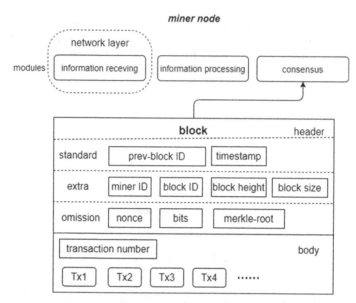

Fig. 4. Detail of miner node and block in bitcoin demo

a series of transactions in mempool into a block, record this block in the node's chain, and send it to the network module with all the remaining miners as the target. In one block, it usually contains the following information: current block ID, current block height, previous block ID, timestamp, miner ID, block size, number of transactions, complete transaction information. In order to save computing power, we did not encrypt and complex verify the content of the block, so there is no Nonce, Bits and Merkle-root in the simulation block header. Each miner node maintains a complete public ledger. In different miner nodes, there may be slight differences in this public ledger. But from the systematic view, it still requires consensus between these ledgers.

2.4 Functions Summary

Through our ChainSim simulation framework described above, ChainSim can provide the following functionality and capability.

- **High number of nodes support in one personal computer.** During historical experiment, simulator can easily afford more than 30k nodes. The cost of high number of nodes is that will use more real time for same simulation time.
- **Flexible transmission mode.** ChainSim can change its transmission mode as unicast, broadcast, multicast, anycast or any special transmission method as we want to set. We can also change the transmission speed for different nodes, which can help us to find out the influence of network status
- **Variable basic parameters.** We can change the basic parameters about the blockchain, such as block size, mining difficulty, miner computing ability, etc.

- *Achieve different protocols.* Based on the overall p2p module, we can achieve different consensus methods and blockchain protocols by defining node behavior. Under the same consensus protocol, we can also define different nodes as different functions. For example, we can set different nodes as fair miner and selfish miner which can be used to reproduce various blockchain attacks.
- *Time-sequence and event-driven.* In ChainSim we can observe the status of any node at any simulation time, also we can observe the response of the whole network after some special command but do not need to stop simulation at that time.

3   Case Study

To verify the correctness and effectiveness of ChainSim, we implemented three different blockchain protocols: Bitcoin, Ethereum and IOTA, then deployed and tested with our ChainSim as case studies.

3.1   Bitcoin

Bitcoin is the most classic blockchain. Next, we will integrate and introduce in detail how we implemented bitcoin under our simulation system.

1)   User node

User node is little affected by different blockchain protocols, mainly produce new transactions and check the historical transaction status. Most of its working mode is presented in Sect. 2.1. Here we will introduce the key parameters we can change in this case study, i.e. user number and the transaction interval. With these two parameters, we can realize the load of the system, which is always statistics as transaction per second (TPS). During our research, in an all good-working system, as all the user nodes do not have much different, the simulation result shows equal between high user nodes number, long interval and low user nodes number, short interval if these two strategy results in a similar TPS. With our ChainSim, we can test the network status and the blockchain response when the system is light load or overload.

2)   Network module

In the bitcoin demo, the main transmission mode is Gossip. The Gossip process is initiated by a seed node. A seed node sends a message to its neighbor nodes in the network. The neighbor nodes that receive the message will repeat the process until all nodes in the network have received the message (Fig. 5).

In ChainSim, the first seed node's work is completed by the consensus module, and the message expansion of Gossip is included in the miner's information process module. In both parts they will send a message with a list of target nodes to the network module. Then network module will distribute it to its goal.

In network module, there is an address book for every single node, including both user nodes and miner nodes. We can set a speed for information transmission in the

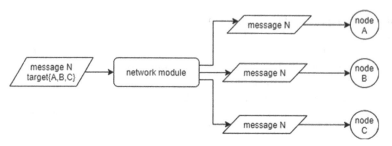

Fig. 5. Network module distributes message

network cable. Then use this speed and the distance between two nodes to calculate first step delay. The second step delay is calculated in the miners information module, which uses the transmission speed and the size of the message. The transmission speed can be set by each node individual. With these settings we can set some nodes with high speed, slow speed network, remote location, etc.

3) **Miner node**

The information processing module are divided into three pieces according to the received information (Fig. 6):

Transaction: Transactions will be verified first. If the transaction is new and valid, it will be put into mempool and wait to be packaged in a new block.

Block: The module will first check whether this block is an unreceived block. If true, compare the height of this block with the block that consensus module is currently mining.

- *Lower:* Just record this block and do nothing.
- *Equal:* Verify this block. If valid, record this block in the blockchain. Then spread this block to several other nodes by sending it in Gossip mode. Finally give the consensus module a command to stop current mining and start a new mining after this new block.
- *Higher:* Which means either this block is invalid or current node has not received past few new blocks. The node will send a request to several nearby nodes to get the blocks between current mining height and the new block height.

Request: Most requests are block synchronization requests from other nodes. Once received, the node will check his blockchain and send the block information back directly. In some cases there will be requests from user nodes to check their transaction status, we didn't include it to reduce the network flow.

The consensus module keeps mining, which means hibernation in our case, at most of the time. When the processing module gives the command of new block. It will add the mining block height first. Then remove all the transactions in the new block out of the mempool. After that, it will find the sixth block before the new block along the

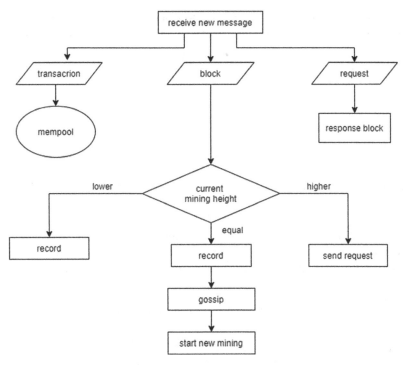

Fig. 6. Information processing module

chain and then confirm it. Next, it will generate a mining time randomly. We obtain this random range by calculating the distribution of real blockchain. We can change the calculating difficulty by changing this distribution. Then the module keeps hibernate. If the mining time finishes and it has not receive the command to mine the next block, we define that this node has successful mined a new block. It will choose the transactions with its working strategy, remove these transactions out of the mempool. At the final step the module will package these transactions and other information as a block, record it in the blockchain and send it to other nodes by gossip. Then it will start a new round of mining.

4) **Verification**

To verify the correctness of our ChainSim, we compared the simulation results with real bitcoin network. All the simulations are running by a single personal computer as shown.

Computer Parameter: **OS:** Windows 10 64 bit
 CPU: Inter® Core™ i7-7700 CPU @ 3.60 GHz
 Memory: 16G
 Programming language: Python 3.6.0
 IDE: JetBrains PyCharm 2019.2.5

Then we decide some parameters for ChainSim bitcoin case before simulation. Some of the parameters have distribution rely on real network, we only show its range in Table 1.

Table 1. Simulation settings.

Parameters	Default	Parameters	Default
Simulation time	24 h	Miner number	2000
Block size	1 MB	Transaction size	[0.4, 2] KB
User number	1000	Mining time	[8, 10] min
Transaction interval	[100, 1000] s	Node transmission speed	[5, 100] Mbps

After simulation, we get the results shown as follows[1].

After comparison, we can find that most of the simulation results are in an acceptable error range, as the real network data is also changing every day (Table 2).

Table 2. Bitcoin network comparison result.

Parameters	Simulation	Real network
Avg block time	548 s	524 s
Avg block size	0.96 MB	1.13 MB
Transaction per second	3.43	3.26
Transaction per block	1640	1836
Mempool size	Depends on time	
Median confirm time	520 s	370 s (with fee)

But there are still some differences between real bitcoin network and simulation, mostly influenced by miner strategy. We limited the block size as 1 MB. In current bitcoin network, SegWit (Segregated Witness) can be chosen by miners to expand block size up to 4 MB, which turns out the average block size can be 1.13 MB or even higher. For mempool size, it is changing all the time in one day. It may be influenced by a sudden congestion of transactions. So it turns out to be incomparable in long time stable simulation. For median confirm time, it is a totally strategy problem and can be further researched. In current simulation, we set all the transactions as no fee, so the miner chooses transactions fairly depend on time. If the user node set a fee in one transaction, how much fee should it contain to make the miner more likely package its transaction first, how many percent of transactions with no fee will one miner package in his block. All these questions can be discussed under our ChainSim.

---

[1] All real blockchain data gets from the following web on April 15, 2020: https://www.blockchain.com/charts, https://bitinfocharts.com/.

In summary, ChainSim shows great ability in simulating a bitcoin network with basic block data and network performance. It is also a great tool for users and miners to find out a better strategy.

3.2 Ethereum

Since Ethereum is still using the POW consensus protocol, it is not modified to POS consensus. Therefore, Ethereum and Bitcoin do not have much different in terms of the operating structure and simulation ideas of the consensus protocol. Based on the Bitcoin simulation case, we made the following two important corrections according to Ethereum unique features.

Uncle Block. If a direct sub-block within 7 layers of the main chain is received, it will no longer be discarded directly, but will be placed in the candidate uncle block. If a new block is mined, miner can add up to two uncle blocks in the current block. When the height difference exceeds 6 layers, or the uncle block is already contained in the uncle field of other blocks, the block is removed from the candidate uncle block (Fig. 7).

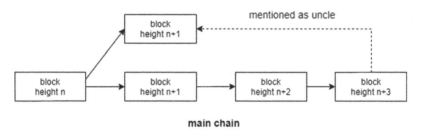

Fig. 7. Uncle block

Smart Contract. As mentioned above, each individual transaction contains some transaction information. We add an identifier to these transactions to distinguish whether this transaction is for currency exchange, building a smart contract or calling a smart contract. In order to implement a single program to run the entire blockchain, smart contracts need to be written in Python syntax instead of Serpent syntax, and can perform operations such as calling the network module to send tokens to an account The entire contract is stored in the transaction information field in a string format. When a miner node receives a request to create a new smart contract account, it will create a separate storage space for the smart contract, decode the string contract and keep the program running, or wait to receive the transaction to call the smart contract. When all the gas in the contract is used, an error status will be reserved in the storage space of the contract, and a new transaction that calls the contract will be fed back with an exception (Fig. 8).

Since Ethereum provides tools for building a private chain, in order to verify the effectiveness of this simulation model, we built a private chain for comparison. The genesis block of private chain is saved in a json document as shown in Fig. 9. Then we generate 4 miner nodes keep mining empty block to test the chain performance.

```
"""from transmissiontype import unicast\nx=x+600\n\
unicast(self.now,self.id,target,transaction,size)"""
```

Fig. 8. Smart contract example

```
1  {
2    "config": {
3      "chainID": 128,
4      "homesteadBlock": 0,
5      "eip155Block": 0,
6      "eip158Block": 0
7    },
8    "alloc": {},
9    "coinbase": "0x0000000000000000000000000000000000000000",
10   "difficulty": "0x400",
11   "extraData": "0x0",
12   "gasLimit": "0x2fefd8",
13   "nonce": "0x000000000000dfa6",
14   "mixhash": "0x0000000000000000000000000000000000000000000000000000000000000000",
15   "parentHash": "0x0000000000000000000000000000000000000000000000000000000000000000",
16   "timestamp": "0x00"
17 }
```

Fig. 9. Private chain genesis block

We compared the simulation results with the real chain and the simulation results with the private chain under the same scale and data volume. The comparison results are as follows:

Table 3. Ethereum comparison result.

Parameters	Simulation	Real network
Avg block time	14 s	13.4 s
Transaction per second	9.42	9
Uncle rate	6.82%	6.16%
Avg block time (private)	14.2 s	13.8 s
Uncle rate (private)	1.31%	1.03%

As shown in Table 3, all the results are similar between simulation and real network. The significant change is that as we only deploy 4 miners in the private chain comparison, uncle rate of the network reduces in a high level, but still almost the same between private chain and simulation.

Similar to the Bitcoin system, except for the impact of transaction incentives on miners choosing to include transactions in blocks, it is not uncommon for Ethereum to have empty blocks in the main chain due to the permission of the appearance of not full even empty blocks. This simulator can also be used as a tool for researching the optimal harvesting strategy of Ethereum miners.

3.3 IOTA

Unlike the previous two chain-structured blockchains, IOTA is a DAG(directed acyclic graph)-structured blockchain. We hope to verify the scalability of our framework through this IOTA demo, and we also tested some user behavior attacks against IOTA in this demo.

In IOTA, its consensus method is named tangle. Instead of the separation process between making transactions by local users and achieving consensus by online miners, tangle integrates these processes into one step. In the iota network, the identities of users and miners overlap, whenever you wish to send a transaction, you need to complete a certain amount of proof of work. We divided the work content of user nodes in IOTA into the following two parts.

1) **Send a transaction**

When the user node attempts to send a transaction, it randomly selects two transactions as the parent transaction from the previous parent transaction pool (the storage space of the DAG structure) based on the weight of the transaction height difference, time difference, verification weight and other factors. Then it executes some proof of work. Package transaction ID, timestamp, transaction height, transaction weight, transaction information, parent transaction and other information into a bundle, and send it to the network module to broadcast it to all nodes.

2) **Receive a transaction**

The user node receives a new bundle and verifies the validity of the transaction in the bundle. If it passes the verification, the transaction is added to the transaction pool. The weight of the parent transaction is superimposed according to the weight and attenuation ratio of this transaction. Then iteratively accumulates the parent transaction weight of the parent transaction. When the weight of a transaction reaches a certain threshold, it is deemed that the transaction has been verified (Fig. 10).

Through the user node working module above, we can easily implement an IOTA simulation and define different types of user behavior patterns to attack the IOTA network. We divide the behavior of users to send transactions into three stages (Table 4):

- *Transaction validity:* Send a transaction with certain validity to reduce the verification difficulty. Invalid transaction means double spending on currency.
- *Selection of parent transaction pool:* That is, the valid transactions received by the node are put into the valid transaction pool, and the invalid transactions enter the invalid transaction pool. User will choose the parent of their new transaction from the selected pool.
- *Parent transaction selection method:* Random selection means that the user node will randomly select the parent transaction in the selected parent transaction pool according to the weight. Selfish selection means that the user node will only select transactions issued by this node or the nodes in the same team.

Through the different combinations of these three stages, we can achieve a variety of attacks on the blockchain. For example, in stage 1, choose to send invalid transactions

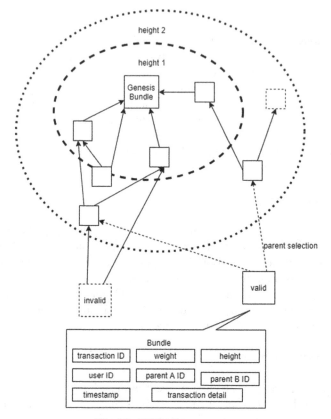

Fig. 10. IOTA demo structure

Table 4. IOTA user behavior

Stage 1	Stage 2	Stage 3
Valid transaction	Valid pool	Random selection
Invalid transaction	Invalid pool	Selfish selection

for double spending, and in stage 2 choose invalid transaction pools to verify double spending transactions, so as to implement double spending attacks. Or selfishly choose to form parasite attack in stage 3. User actions at different stages can appear randomly and proportionally to change the attack intensity.

After testing, it was found that the parasitic attack caused by selfish behavior has a limited impact on the normal operation of the overall DAG structure blockchain. More malicious nodes and a higher attack rate will significantly increase the absolute number of invalid transactions, but does not increase the success rate of the attack (i.e. invalid transactions are verified). From an overall perspective, the DAG structure of IOTA is stable. Specific research data will be released in the future paper.

At the same time, we also found that there are more contents that can be studied in the current IOTA simulation demo. For example, the difficulty of proof of work when sending a transaction (the time it takes); when selecting the parent transaction, the importance of the transaction height difference, time difference, verification weight and other factors; the attenuation ratio of the parent transaction weight iteration. The impact of these factors will be the goal of our future research.

4 Related Work

Given the advantage of blockchain simulation, a few blockchain simulators have been developed. We discuss these related work as follows:

Maher et al. [5] organized their simulator in three layers: incentive layer, connector layer and system layer. The connector layer is the core part of the simulator, which includes the consensus algorithm, mostly POW in this paper. They allow simulating a large number of nodes to study the behavior of the nodes and the incentive mechanisms. But they have already defined and locked the working mode of the miners which means miners are all assumed to be honest. They must append as many transactions as they can in one single block and the transactions that offer the highest fees must be included first. They also add an extra new vote mechanism to resolve fork instead of upgrading the copy of the chain by the miner himself.

Lyubomir et al. [6] design their simulator to explore important characteristics and metrics of the network, reason about interactions between nodes, and compare different scenarios in an intuitive way. It shows the simulation time usage comparison as the transaction number changes. It can also simulate large amounts of nodes in one single personal computer. In their simulator, they mostly focus on the transaction sending and network response to replicate the parallel and concurrent nature of the network. But as a blockchain simulator, instead of a network simulator, it weakens the consensus part, which is more important in blockchain.

Yusuke et al. [7] produce a simulator which can simulate the block transmission with good accuracy. They conduct two experiments which clarify the influence of neighbor node selection algorithms and relay networks on the block propagation time. In their simulator, they ignore the transactions generator, which always equals to users, just starting the simulation from block level. To speed up the simulation time, they simulate all the messages as 0 byte except the block message. As they try to change the transmission protocol to decrease block propagation time, they set an unchangeable consensus PoW as well.

5 Conclusion and Future Work

In this paper, we present our P2P blockchain simulation framework: ChainSim[2]. We describe in detail how this simulator works, and deploy three types of blockchain protocols demo under this framework. The simulation results shows that our simulator

---

[2] ChainSim will be released as open source soon.

could simulate the blockchain accurate and effective in one single computer. Also, it can change different parameter and strategies to realize different kinds of attack in blockchain. ChainSim can be used by either researchers to test and evaluate their new consensus protocols, or blockchain foundations to predicate and plan their resources for their blockchains before deployment.

As future work, we will improve our simulation framework, test more network influence causing by different miner work strategies and try to improve the performance of blockchain by changing parameters or testing new protocols.

References

1. Nakamoto, S.: Bitcoin: a peer-to-peer electronic cash system (2008). https://bitcoin.org/bit coin.pdf
2. Buterin, V.: Ethereum white paper. GitHub repository 1, pp. 22–23 (2013)
3. Androulaki, E., et al.: Hyperledger fabric: a distributed operating system for permissioned blockchains. In: Proceedings of the Thirteenth EuroSys Conference, pp. 1–15 (2018)
4. Popov, S.: The Tangle. IOTA White Paper (2017). https://www.iota.org/
5. Alharby, M., van Moorsel, A.: BlockSim: a simulation framework for blockchain systems. ACM SIGMETRICS Perform. Eval. Rev. 46(3), 135–138 (2019)
6. Stoykov, L., Zhang, K., Jacobsen, H.-A.: VIBES: fast blockchain simulations for large-scale peer-to-peer networks. In: Proceedings of the 18th ACM/IFIP/USENIX Middleware Conference: Posters and Demos, pp. 19–20 (2017)
7. Aoki, Y., Otsuki, K., Kaneko, T., Banno, R., Shudo, K.: SimBlock: a blockchain network simulator. In: IEEE INFOCOM 2019-IEEE Conference on Computer Communications Workshops, pp. 325–329 (2019)
8. Göbel, J., Krzesinski, A.E.: Increased block size and Bitcoin blockchain dynamics. In: 2017 27th International Telecommunication Networks and Applications Conference, pp. 1–6 (2017)
9. Memon, R.A., Li, J.P., Ahmed, J.: Simulation model for blockchain systems using queuing theory. Electronics 8(2), 234 (2019)
10. Yasaweerasinghelage, R., Staples, M., Weber, I.: Predicting latency of blockchain-based systems using architectural modelling and simulation. In: 2017 IEEE International Conference on Software Architecture, pp. 253–256 (2017)
11. Goswami, S.: Scalability analysis of Blockchains through Blockchain simulation (2017). https://digitalscholarship.unlv.edu/thesesdissertations/2976/
12. Chen, C., Qi, Z., Liu, Y., Lei, K.: Using virtualization for blockchain testing. In: Qiu, M. (ed.) SmartCom 2017. LNCS, vol. 10699, pp. 289–299. Springer, Cham (2018). https://doi.org/10.1007/978-3-319-73830-7_29
13. Gervais, A., Karame, G.O., Wüst, K., Glykantzis, V., Ritzdorf, H., Capkun, S.: On the security and performance of proof of work blockchains. In: Proceedings of the 2016 ACM SIGSAC Conference on Computer and Communications Security, pp. 3–16 (2016)
14. Sompolinsky, Y., Zohar, A.: Secure high-rate transaction processing in bitcoin. In: Böhme, R., Okamoto, T. (eds.) FC 2015. LNCS, vol. 8975, pp. 507–527. Springer, Heidelberg (2015). https://doi.org/10.1007/978-3-662-47854-7_32

Blockchain-Based Access Control Mechanism in Electronic Evidence

Yunjia Zhang, Jian Wang$^{(\boxtimes)}$, Xudong He, and Jiqiang Liu

Beijing Key Laboratory of Security and Privacy in Intelligent Transportation,
Beijing Jiaotong University, Beijing, China
wangjian@bjtu.edu.cn

Abstract. With rapid development of the information age, the proportion of electronic evidence involved in judicial cases has been rising, and the importance of electronic evidence is increasingly prominent. In the real judicial process, there are strict requirements put forward for the authenticity identification, tamper proof storage and legal sharing methods of electronic evidence, bringing many security challenges. If such conditions are not met, the legal force of electronic evidence will be seriously reduced. However, the existing technical solutions can not meet these above requirements. Blockchain technology has the characteristics of decentralization and tamper proof, which provides a new method for the storage and extraction of electronic evidence. To solve these problems, this paper proposes a blockchain-based storage access control model for electronic evidence and designs the corresponding storage access control protocol. In this scheme, multi-entity cooperation is allowed to store evidence, and a zero-knowledge proof protocol is applied to achieve access control and data sharing. Through the security and experimental analysis, it can be proved that the scheme satisfies security features such as known key security and non-repudiation, and can effectively resist collusion, camouflage, replay and man-in-the-middle attacks. Finally, related experiments show that the scheme has high computational and communication efficiency. In this way, the problem of secure storage and sharing of electronic evidence will be resolved commendably, which meets the security requirements in actual scene.

Keywords: Block chain · Electronic evidence · Access control · Zero-knowledge proof · CP-ABE

1 Introduction

In the wake of comprehensive popularization of computer technology and rapid development of digital economy, the services, transactions and business processes

Supported by Major Scientific and Technological Innovation Projects of Shandong Province, China (No. 2019JZZY020128) and the Fundamental Research Funds for the Central Universities (2019YJS033).

© Springer Nature Singapore Pte Ltd. 2021
K. Xu et al. (Eds.): CBCC 2020, CCIS 1305, pp. 17–33, 2021.
https://doi.org/10.1007/978-981-33-6478-3_2

of various industries have gradually shifted from offline to online. According to the 45th "China Statistical Report on Internet Development" released by China Internet Network Information Center, as of March 2020, there were 710 million online shopping users and 694 million online government service users in China, which grown by 76.3% compared with end of 2018 [1]. Based on this trend, with the help of laws and regulations, the application of electronic contracts is becoming more and more extensive. It is demonstrated by iimedia research that the number of electronic contracts signed in China is expected to exceed 50 billion times in 2020, with a year-on-year growth rate of 317.5%. This shows that electronic files have come to be the main carrier for people to transmit information and record facts. While data turns into an important asset, the types and fields of legal disputes also undergo significant changes. Electronic data has become the most common form of evidence in judicial trial process. In the light of analysis on China Judgements Online [2], about 90% of intellectual property civil judgments have involved electronic evidence[3] in the past three years. It can be seen that electronic evidence is increasingly diversified in judicial practice, moving toward trends such as large quantity, rapid growth, high proportion, and wide variety. The judicial system has entered the era of electronic evidence from physical evidence [4].

Although electronic evidence has been widely used, due to its own properties such as diversity, virtuality and ease of falsifying, it still faces many challenges in judicial practice. Primarily in terms of storage, the traditional method of evidence storage by single entity is not only hard to ensure the authenticity and reliability of evidence, but also extremely easy to result in data modification or loss, whose process is difficult to trace. Moreover, since electronic evidence needs to be shared among multiple entities in the judicial process, the access role must be rigorously controlled in this process to ensure legal extraction of electronic evidence for fear of malicious access and use. Therefore, it is urgent to design an efficient storage access control mechanism for electronic evidence to solve these problems, enhancing its admissibility and probative Force [5].

As a distributed shared database, blockchain technology has the characteristics of decentralization, tamper-resistance and traceability [6,7], which can be applied to meet the access requirements of electronic evidence. However, the data privacy on the chain is facing challenges owing to the openness and transparency of blockchain [8]. At present, most of related research only aim at storing electronic evidence on the blockchain, without reasonable access control and secure sharing of evidence, lacking attention to the data privacy. In addition, there are still single-point trust issues in these work, which cannot highly guarantee the authenticity, integrity, privacy, and traceability of evidence in its life cycle. Based on this, this paper will consider blockchain-based storage access control mechanism for electronic evidence to make up for the above-mentioned shortcomings and satisfy the actual demand.

The main contributions of this paper are as follows: Above all, a storage access control model for electronic evidence is established. This model is composed of two blockchains (judicial consortium chain and evidence chain) and an off-chain database. While realizing storage and access functions, it can manage data more distinctly and reduce local storage cost, without the single-point trust issue.

Furthermore, based on the proposed model, a storage access control protocol for electronic evidence is designed. The protocol permits multi-entity cooperation to encrypt and store data in a collaborative way on chain and off chain, and realizes access control and data sharing through a multi-node zero-knowledge proof protocol.

At last, the security and performance analysis of this scheme is carried out. It is proved that the work in this paper fulfills secure storage and sharing of electronic evidence, which can guarantee its authenticity, integrity, privacy and traceability, and resist collusion, camouflage, replay and man-in-the-middle attacks. Related experiments show that this scheme is enough to adapt to actual background with high computational and communication efficiency.

The rest of the paper is structured as follows: Sect. 2 overviews the related work. In Sect. 3, an access model based on blockchain for electronic evidence is established, and the implementation process of the scheme under this model is explained in detail. Then the security and performance analysis is carried out in Sect. 4. Finally, Sect. 5 draws conclusions.

2   Related Work

At present, some scholars have applied blockchain technology to the research of electronic evidence. In 2019, G. Maciá-Fernández et al. paid attention to the risks existing in current network behaviors, and proposed an idea to preserve the evidence generated from network behaviors in a blockchain-based platform, so as to maintain its invariance [9]. Based on this situation, Xiong yu et al. built an electronic evidence access model using blockchain, which aimed to satisfy the preservation and backup demand in the process of the last step from extraction to presentation of evidence in court [10]. Nevertheless, the model does not ensure the authenticity of electronic evidence on the chain, while lacking specific access control methods and behavioral constraints on the central database. In the case where the ownership of electronic evidence needs to undergo multiple changes at different stages of judicial process, Silvia Bonomi et al. described a blockchain-based chain of custody for evidences management in digital forensics [11]. Although falsification of evidence has been curbed, this scheme does not identify the evidence on the chain and there is no confidentiality measure about the off-chain database, leading to a centralized problem. Moreover, Zhihong Tian et al. proposed a secure electronic evidence framework based on blockchain, which uses multilevel encryption schemes to protect the privacy and traceability of evidence [12]. However, this approach relies on the honesty of the third-party storage service provider, lacks attention to its malicious behaviors and requires a centralized certification authority to generate key pairs, which results in the authority trust problem. As the reliability of electronic evidence is reduced by centralized collection and storage, Mehra pourvahab et al. proposed a digital forensics architecture for evidence collection and provenance preservation in

IaaS cloud environment using SDN and blockchain technology [13]. Similarly, the scheme involves a trusted third party for identity authentication and key generation, and there is also an authority trust problem.

In addition, in the centralized storage mode of electronic data, for the purpose of preventing cloud service providers or malicious attackers from gaining control of data [14], some scholars have considered access control methods in cloud environment based on blockchain to protect the privacy and integrity of data [15–19]. Among them, M.Jemel et al. employed CP-ABE [20] with time dimension to control the access rights of users in the process of cloud data sharing. In other scenarios like medical services, there are also some researches which combine blockchain technology with access control, such as the blockchain-based access control scheme for electronic medical records [21].

In order to make up for the shortcomings of current blockchain-based electronic evidence access solution, the solution constructed in this paper is not limited to tamper-proof storage of electronic evidence, but also the guarantee of its authenticity and validity on the chain, and contains a secure and reliable access control mechanism. When designing the scheme, this paper fully considers the malicious behaviors that may be produced by the third-party database, thereby ensuring integrity and privacy of data. Furthermore, there is not any centralized organization for issuing certificates or keys, which avoids single-point trust issues well.

3   Proposed Access Control Mechanism

This section describes the access control mechanism of electronic evidence proposed in this paper which consists of two parts: an access control model and the specific implementation process of the protocol under this model.

3.1   Access Control Model of Electronic Evidence

Combined with blockchain technology, the model is built to ensure that all entities in the judicial process always make correct submission, secure storage and reliable access of evidence. How to build the model is shown in Fig. 1, containing four parts.

Users. Users in the model are the entities participating in judicial process, mainly involving authoritative users such as procuratorate, public security organ, court, and the third-party users such as notary office, appraisal center and arbitration agency. It should be noted that the submission of electronic evidence to the chain is completed by authoritative users as owners. Before that, the third-party users can identify relevant evidence and give their opinions as collaborators. As the nodes in the blockchain network, all users maintain the chain together.

Judicial Consortium Chain (JudChain). JudChain mainly stores transaction and cooperation data between node users, which is accurate to trace their behaviors in judicial process.

Evidence Chain (EviChain). EviChain stores the electronic evidence information generated by authoritative nodes, mainly including the case number of electronic evidence, the encrypted value of relevant metadata, and the user identifiers that are permitted to access the evidence. The metadata includes the owner, type, name, signature, time, place, participants and hash value of the electronic evidence.

Off-Chain Database (OffchainDB). This database uses hash value of electronic evidence as index to store ciphertext form and access policy of complete electronic evidence, which is serviced by a third party.

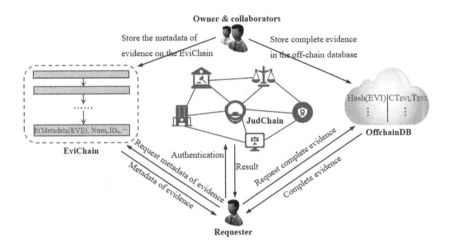

Fig. 1. The blockchain-based access model of electronic evidence.

3.2 Access Control Protocol of Electronic Evidence

This part details the steps for implementation of this protocol, whose definition of relevant symbols is shown in Table 1 and workflow is shown in Fig. 2.

Initialization. A node P applies to join the blockchain network, selects a large prime number q, the generator g of Z_q^* and a random number x_p ($1 < x_p < q\text{-}1$) as its private key and calculates $y_p = g^{x_p} \bmod q$ as the public key. Based on the discrete logarithm problem, it is difficult to recover the private key from

Table 1. Symbol definition.

Symbol	Definition
$Owner_i$	Owner of evidence i
$Requester_i$	Requester of evidence i
x_i	Private key of user i
y_i	Public key of user i
SK_i	Attribute-based private key of user i
ID_i	Identifier of user i
Sig_i	Digital signature of user i
$Hash(i)$	Hash value of i
NUM_i	Identifier of case i (case number)
K_i	Symmetric key of case i
$Metadata(i)$	Metadata of electronic evidence i
$TYPE_i$	Type of electronic evidence i
$NAME_i$	Name of electronic evidence i
$TIME_i$	Generation time of electronic evidence i
POS_i	Generation location of evidence i
$PARTIES_i$	Participants involved in evidence i
T_i	Access policy of electronic evidence i
$Encrypted(i)$	Encrypted value of i
C_i/CT_i	Ciphertext of i

the public key. Finally, P broadcasts its identification and public key y_p to the blockchain network.

After receiving the request information of P, every authoritative node V_i in the network verifies its identity and the existence of y_p in JudChain to ensure the uniqueness of its certificate. If the authentication is passed and the public key y_p has not been stored locally before, the corresponding ID_P will be generated for node P according to the system rules. V_i broadcasts ID_P.

If every V_i passes its authentication request and generates the same ID_P, node P is joined successfully, that is, x_p, y_p and ID_P take effect. All nodes update the blockchain (y_p and ID_P are added to their local storage).

Additionally, if node P is an authoritative node, it will execute the setup algorithm of attribute-based encryption [22] to generate the common parameters needed for encrypting electronic evidence: input the number of system attributes U, a group G with prime order r, the generator o of G, and the random numbers $h_1, \ldots\ldots, h_U \in G$ related to the U system attributes. Moreover, P randomly selects α, $\beta \in Z_r$ and calculates the public key $PK = o, e(o,o)^\alpha, o^\beta, h_1, \ldots\ldots, h_U$, where $e()$ represents a bilinear operation. The master key $MSK = o^\alpha$.

Store the Metadata on the EviChain. The authoritative node P(joined the blockchain network in the initialization step) owns an electronic evidence EVI, whose case number is NUM_j. This paper assumes that nodes P_2, P_3 and P_4 participate in the notarization or identification of EVI, and the metadata of it called $Metadata(EVI) = (Owner_p||Type_{EVI}||Name_{EVI}||Sig_{P_2}||Sig_{P_3}||Sig_{P_4}||Time_{EVI}||Pos_{EVI}||Parties_{EVI}||Hash(EVI))$. P selects a key K_j for case j, encrypts $Metadata(EVI)$ using symmetric encryption algorithm with K_j, and decides the user identifier that can access EVI such as ID_W. Finally, $encrypted(metadata(EVI))$, ID_W and NUM_j are stored in the block of EviChain.

Store the Complete Evidence in the OffchainDB. This paper improves the details of CP-ABE algorithm proposed in [22] to make it suitable for our scenario.

Node P formulates the access policy T_{EVI} of EVI: an $m \times n$ LSSS matrix, where the ith row t_i is associated with attribute j, $i \in [1,......,m]$. The function ρ maps the row t_i to the attribute j, i.e.$\rho : \{1,......,m\} \rightarrow \{1,......,U\}$. After that, P divides T_{EVI} into row disjoint submatrices namely T_2, T_3 and T_4 , which are assigned to P_2, P_3 and P_4 respectively. Meanwhile, P randomly selects s, $s*c$, $y_2, ..., y_n \in Z_r^n$ and sends the column vector $v = (s*c, y_2, ..., y_n)$ to P_2, P_3 and P_4.

P calculates the ciphertext $C_{EVI} = EVI * e(o,o)^{\alpha s}$, $C'_{EVI} = o^{s*c}$.

P_2, P_3 and P_4 execute respectively: for the assigned submatrix $T_{2/3/4}(d \times n, 1 < d < m)$, where the ith row t_i is associated with attribute j, $i \in D = [1,......,d]$, they calculate $\forall i \in [1,......,d]$ $\lambda_i = t_i v$, indicating the share of secret sharing key. After that, they select random numbers $r_1,......,r_d \in Z_r$, compute $\forall i \in [1,......,d]$ $C_i = o^{\beta\lambda_i} h_{\rho(i)}^{-r_i}$, $D_i = o^{r_i}$ and send them to P.

At last, P uses $Hash(EVI)$ as index to store $CT_{EVI} = (C_{EVI}, C'_{EVI}, \forall i \in [1,......,m](C_i, D_i))$ and the access policy T_{EVI} in OffchainDB.

Authentication of the Requester on the Chain (Zero-Knowledge Proof Protocol). According to the target case number NUM_j, node W searches all evidence related to the case on EviChain, and sends a data request to trigger the smart contract for authentication. When W requests authentication for the first time, it computes $n_i = y_{P_i}^{x_w} \bmod q$ and saves n_i locally as the two-way validation parameter when constructing zero knowledge commitment to the authoritative node P_i.

W selects a random number $a(1 < a < q-1)$, calculates $b = g^a \bmod q$, $z_i = (a + x_w - Hash(b, ID_w)*n_i)\bmod(q-1)$ and broadcasts (ID_W, NUM_j, z_i, b, t), where t is the generation timestamp of the commitment.

After receiving (ID_W, NUM_j, z_i, b, t) at time t', P_i confirms that $t' - t < \triangle t$, b appears for the first time in the commitments of W, and whether ID_W is the identifier that is permitted to access relevant evidence on the EviChain. Then it verifies whether the equation $b * y_w = g^{z_i + Hash(b, ID'_w)*n'_i} \bmod q$ is true.

Δt is the allowed message delay in the system, and ID'_W is the identifier of W stored locally by node Pi. $n'_i = y_w^{x_{p_i}} \bmod q$.

If each validation node P_i obtains the equal and correct verification result, the authentication of W will pass successfully. Afterwards, the owner of evidence, P, broadcasts the case key as $key = K_j * (y_w^{x_p} \bmod q)$. W calculates $K'_j = key * (y_p^{x_w} \bmod q)^{-1}$ and decrypts the metadata of evidence related to the case j with K'_j to gain the metadata plaintext.

Generate Private Key for Requester. After W passes authentication on the chain, based on the metadata content obtained in the previous step, it determines the specific target evidence EVI it aims to obtain and issues the request. The key generation algorithm in [22] is improved. At this time, owner P generates the attribute private key for W according to the attribute set S of W: selects a random number $t \in Z_r$, calculates $SK_w = (E = o^{\alpha c^{-1}} o^{\beta t}, L = o^t, \forall i \in S \; E_i = h_i^t)$ and send SK_w to W.

Requestor Obtains Complete Electronic Evidence. W obtains the encrypted value of complete electronic evidence EVI from OffchainDB and calculates

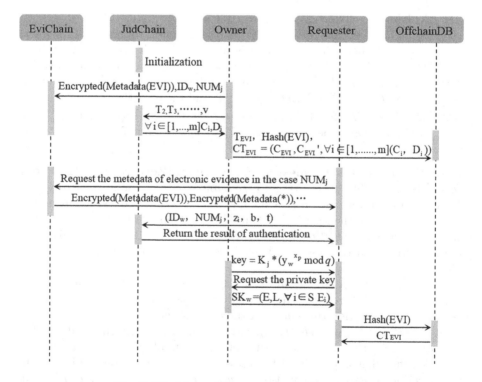

Fig. 2. Workflow of the access control protocol.

$e(C'_{EVI}, E)/(\prod_{i \in I} (e(C_i, L)e(D_i, E_{\rho(i)}))^{\omega_i}) = e(o, o)^{\alpha s} e(o, o)^{\beta sct}/(\prod_{i \in I}$
$e(o, o)^{t\beta\lambda_i\omega_i}) = e(o, o)^{\alpha s}$, $EVI' = C_{EVI}/e(o, o)^{\alpha s}$, which is the improved decryption algorithm in [22]. Besides, W can calculate $Hash(EVI')$ and compare it with $Hash(EVI)$ in the metadata of EVI on EviChain. If they are equal, it means that the evidence EVI has not been tampered with in OffchainDB.

4 Security and Performance Analysis

This section will analyze the protocol proposed in this paper, which is divided into two parts: security analysis and performance analysis.

4.1 Security Analysis

The Correctness of the Zero-Knowledge Proof Protocol.

- Non-interactivity: In the non-interactive form, the prover and verifier need to have a common short random string called reference string instead of interaction. Moreover, the decision right of the random string cannot be handed over to the prover. Here, this protocol uses the random string $c = Hash(b, ID_W) * n_i$. If the malicious prover visits the hash random oracle for d times to obtain a specific value, the probability that he can get the correct hash value is only $d/2^m$ (m is the size of target space mapped by the hash function), which is a very small probability. In addition, in order to pass the authentication successfully, the prover can only use specific ID_W and n_i, and only the parameter b controlled by parameter a can be determined by himself. In this case, it is almost impossible to get a specific value.
- Zero knowledge: In this agreement, the verifier uses commitment z_i, public key y_w, shared parameter b and random string $c' = hash(b, ID'_W) * n'_i$ to verify the identity of prover, so as to believe that he is the legal owner of identity identifier ID_W and private key x_w. However, due to the difficulty of random numbers collision and discrete logarithms, the probability of the recovering the prover's private key from these parameters can be ignored for verifier.
- Correctness: Honest provers and verifiers are always able to successfully implement the protocol. The algorithm process is as follows:
    Condition 1. The prover W and verifier P_i of commitment z_i can be legally corresponding, i.e. $n_i = n'_i$.
    Condition 2. The prover W has a legal identity with access rights, that is, $y_w = g^{x_w} \bmod q$ and $ID_W = ID'_W$.
    The verifier P_i performs $g^{z_i + Hash(b, ID'_W) * n'_i} \equiv g^{a + x_w - Hash(b, ID_W) * n_i + Hash(b, ID'_W) * n'_i} \equiv g^a * g^{x_w} \equiv b * y_w \bmod q$.

The Security Analysis of This Scheme.

- Decentralization: In this network, the relationship between nodes is equal, and there is no central authority. Therefore, there will not be failures of a single point or attacks on the central server that will paralyze the entire network service, reducing the security risk of the network. At the same time, this method avoids the central server from monopolizing, snooping or tampering with the data, and can protect the privacy of users.
- Secure storage and extraction: The storage mode is based on the multi-party cooperative encryption method, that is, the storage of an evidence is determined by multiple nodes rather than a user, thus ensuring the authenticity and validity of the stored evidence. The access mode adopts the form of two-level control: user can obtain the attribute private key and decrypt the index value off the chain after passing the authentication on the chain, so as to retrieve and decrypt the complete evidence according to the policy in the off-chain database, which realizes access control of the evidence securely. It should be noted that the general attribute-based encryption scheme directly distributes the key according to the attributes submitted by the user. In this paper, the authenticity of these attributes is verified first, and then the key is distributed to user, thus increasing the security of access control scheme.
- Authenticity: The plaintext of metadata on the chain contains multi-party signatures, that is, multi-party nodes jointly determine whether the evidence can be stored on the chain. As long as the decrypted signature is compared with the hash value, the user can verify the authenticity of the evidence on the chain. In addition, the authenticity of off-chain evidence is verified by comparing the consistency of the hash value of complete evidence off and on the chain.
- Indistinguishability: The storage structure of electronic evidence on the chain is the encrypted value of metadata, which is hashed and encrypted symmetrically. If an unauthorized person does not have the decryption key, he cannot distinguish the target evidence. In addition, the storage structure of evidence in off-chain database is the encrypted value indexed by hash value of it. Without successful authentication, the user cannot obtain the index, and based on the indistinguishability of hash algorithm, the evidence stored in the database cannot be distinguished.
- Security of known key: The on-chain protocol adopts the method of one case one secret kry, that is, the electronic evidences of different cases are encrypted and decrypted by different keys. If the key of a case is leaked carelessly, the keys of other cases will not be affected, so the security hazard caused by key disclosure is limited to the range of the current case. Moreover, even if the disclosure only divulges the metadata of the evidence of the case, the complete evidence off the chain will not be affected.
- Anti-collusion attack: The encryption of evidence needs to be completed by the cooperation of n nodes, and any nodes $< n$ cannot successfully encrypt and store it. Therefore, the protocol can prevent collusion storage with $n-1$-scale. In addition, in the zero-knowledge authentication protocol, there are m

authentication nodes to authenticate the requester respectively. If and only if all m nodes complete the authentication successfully, the user is a legal requester. Therefore, the protocol can resist collusion attack with $m-1$-scale.

- Bidirectional authentication with non-repudiation: In the zero-knowledge proof protocol, requester W uses the two-way secret parameter $n_i = y_{p_i}^{x_w} \bmod q$ when constructing the commitment z_i, and verifier P_i uses the parameter $n_i' = y_w^{x_{p_i}} \bmod q$ when verifying its commitment, obviously $n_i = n_i'$. In other words, the requester and verifier are unique for a particular commitment. In addition, after the requester passes authentication, the owner P of evidence uses parameter $y_w^{x_p} \bmod q$ to share the key with W, and W uses $y_p^{x_w} \bmod q$ to decrypt the shared key. The above parameters can only be calculated by specific users, that is to say, both parties can authenticate each other in the authentication or secret key sharing stage, and the authentication has non-repudiation.

- Unforgeability: If an attacker tries to impersonate a node P, he must obtain his private key x_p. However, if he wants to recover x_p from the public key y_p, he has to face the problem of discrete logarithm. Similarly, in order to recover x_p from the commitment constructed by node P, even if the verifier's private key is known and the secret parameter n is calculated, it is still necessary to obtain the random parameter a in the commitment and the problem of discrete logarithm has to be solved in the recovery of parameter a. Therefore, the users in this protocol can not be forged.

  In addition, the off-chain ciphertext of evidence is constructed by the cooperation of multiple nodes, and the sub ciphertext is calculated by random numbers selected by the node itself, which are not transmitted through the network and known by other nodes.

- Anti-replay attack: In the zero-knowledge authentication protocol, if an attacker replays the commitment constructed by a requester to the network, the verifier will also refuse to pass the authentication due to the restriction of timestamp and the repetition of random number. Even if individual nodes are successfully spoofed, it is difficult for attacker to guarantee that all verification nodes can be cheated. Therefore, the protocol can resist replay attack.

- Anti-man-in-the-middle attack: In the zero-knowledge authentication protocol, the communication between nodes does not need the third party to forward, so there is no case that the third party is attacked and results in data tampering. Even if the attacker intercepts a message in the network and tampers with it, it is difficult to make all receivers believe its authenticity and validity within the specified time, so as to achieve no attack effect. Therefore, the protocol can prevent the message from being tampered and resist man-in-the-middle attack.

The security comparison results between this paper and references [12] and [15] are shown in Table 2.

Table 2. Security comparison results.

Contrast parameters	This paper	[12]	[15]
Decentralization	√	×	√
Secure storage and extraction	√	×	√
Authenticity	√	√	×
Indistinguishability	√	×	×
Security of known key	√	×	√
Anti-collusion attack	√	√	√
Bidirectional authentication	√	×	√
Non-repudiation	√	√	√
Unforgeability	√	√	√
Anti-replay attack	√	×	√
Anti-man-in-the-middle attack	√	√	√

4.2   Performance Analysis

In this part, the performance simulation experiment of the proposed protocol is carried out, and a comparative analysis is made between this protocol, literature [12] and literature [15] in terms of computing cost and communication cost.

Here, this paper stipulates that in the three schemes, the number of data encryption participants is n, and the number of verification nodes in the blockchain is t. The calculation amount of the whole protocol is shown in Table 3. The related overhead parameters of each operation and communication are from reference [23].

Computation Cost. Firstly, this paper compares the relationship between the number of blockchain nodes and the computation cost in three schemes, assuming $n = 2$ (the minimum number of encryption participants). The results are shown in Fig. 3. It can be seen that the computation cost of our scheme is significantly lower than that in reference [15]. When the number of nodes increases to a certain value, our computation cost is slightly higher than that in reference [12]. The reason is that in order to achieve a higher security strength, this paper uses multiple modular and exponential operations.

Since there is no data encryption participant in reference [12], we compare the relationship between the number of encryptors and the computation cost in this scheme and reference [15]. Assuming $t = 2$ (the minimum number of blockchain nodes), the result is shown in Fig. 4. It can be seen that with the increase of the number of encryption participants, the computation cost of our scheme is significantly lower than that in reference [15].

Communication Cost. This part compares the communication cost of the three schemes according to their data interaction modes and message length.

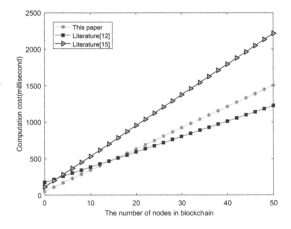

Fig. 3. Relationship between the number of nodes in blockchain and the computation cost.

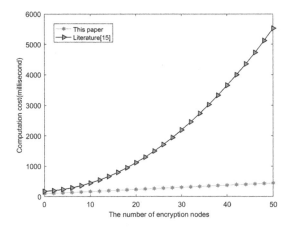

Fig. 4. Relationship between the number of encryption nodes and the computation cost.

Similar to the computation cost, we first assume $n = 2$ and compare the relationship between the number of blockchain nodes and communication cost in the three schemes. The results are shown in Fig. 5. It can be seen that the communication cost of our scheme is less than that of the other two schemes, and with the increase of the number of blockchain nodes, the difference becomes more and more obvious.

Next, we assume $t = 2$ to compare the relationship between the number of encryptors and communication cost in our scheme and reference [15]. As shown in Fig. 6, with the increase of the number of encryption participants, the communication cost of us is much lower than that in reference [15].

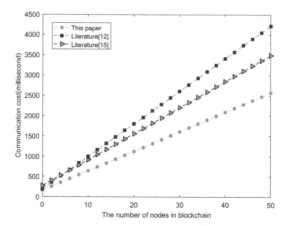

Fig. 5. Relationship between the number of nodes in blockchain and the communication cost.

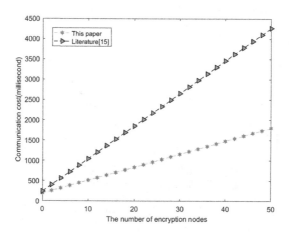

Fig. 6. Relationship between the number of encryption nodes and the communication cost.

Table 3. Calculation amount of three schemes.

Calculation amount	This paper	[12]	[15]
Hash	$2 + 3t$	$3 + t$	$7 + 2t$
Random number	$5 + n$	0	n
Symmetric encryption/decryption	2	0	2
Modular/exponential operation	$13 + 3t + 3n$	0	$2n^2 - 4n + 2$
Bilinear operation	4	0	0
Signature/verification	$2t$	$17 + 2t$	$8 + 4t + n$

It should be noted that the values of t and n assumed in this paper when comparing the cost of the three schemes only determine the size of the curve base, and will not affect slope and change trend of the curve. Therefore, it is effective to compare and analyze the performance of three schemes.

5 Conclusion

This paper proposes a blockchain-based access control mechanism for electronic evidence, which mainly contains a storage access control model and a corresponding storage access control protocol. This mechanism allows multi-entity cooperation to encrypt and store data to ensure the authenticity and privacy of the data on the chain. A new zero-knowledge proof protocol is applied to control access rights and share data. In addition, we combine and improve CP-ABE algorithm to protect the integrity of evidence and prevent the malicious behaviors of the third party. It should be noted that this mechanism does not require any centralized certification authority to provide key generation services, thus avoiding the centralization problem. The related security analysis and experiments show that the proposed mechanism has non-repudiation and guarantees the security of known keys, which can effectively resist collusion, camouflage, replay and man-in-the-middle attacks with high computational and communication efficiency.

Acknowledgement. This work was supported in part by Major Scientific and Technological Innovation Projects of Shandong Province, China (No. 2019JZZY020128) and the Fundamental Research Funds for the Central Universities(2019YJS033).

References

1. Office of the Central Cyberspace Affairs Commission. The 45th China statistical report on internet development (2020). http://www.cac.gov.cn/2020-04/27/c_1589535470378587.htm
2. The Supreme People's Court of The People's Republic of China. China judgements online (2020). http://wenshu.court.gov.cn
3. Volonino, L.: Computer forensics and electronic evidence. In: 9th Americas Conference on Information Systems, AMCIS 2003, Tampa, FL, USA, 4–6 August 2003, p. 426. Association for Information Systems (2003)
4. Losavio, M., Adams, J., Rogers, M.: Gap analysis: judicial experience and perception of electronic evidence. J. Digit. Forensic Pract. 1(1), 13–17 (2006)
5. Insa, F.: The admissibility of electronic evidence in court (A.E.E.C.): fighting against high-tech crime - results of a European study. J. Digit. Forensic Pract. 1(4), 285–289 (2006)
6. Nakamoto, S.: Bitcoin: a peer-to-peer electronic cash system (2008)
7. Kosba, A.E., Miller, A., Shi, E., Wen, Z., Papamanthou, C.: Hawk: the blockchain model of cryptography and privacy-preserving smart contracts. In: IEEE Symposium on Security and Privacy, SP 2016, San Jose, CA, USA, 22–26 May 2016, pp. 839–858. IEEE Computer Society (2016)

8. Karame, G.: On the security and scalability of bitcoin's blockchain. In: Weippl, E.R., Katzenbeisser, S., Kruegel, C., Myers, A.C., Halevi, S. (eds.) Proceedings of the 2016 ACM SIGSAC Conference on Computer and Communications Security, Vienna, Austria, 24–28 October 2016, pp. 1861–1862. ACM (2016)

9. Maciá-Fernández, G., Antonio Gómez-Hernández, J., Robles, M., García-Teodoro, P.: Blockchain-based forensic system for collection and preservation of network service evidences. Digit. Investig. **28**(Supplement), S141 (2019)

10. Xiong, Y., Du, J.: Electronic evidence preservation model based on blockchain. In: Wang, Y., Chang, C.-C. (eds.) Proceedings of the 3rd International Conference on Cryptography, Security and Privacy. ICCSP 2019, Kuala Lumpur, Malaysia, 19–21 January 2019, pp. 1–5. ACM (2019)

11. Bonomi, S., Casini, M., Ciccotelli, C.: B-CoC: a blockchain-based chain of custody for evidences management in digital forensics. CoRR, abs/1807.10359 (2018)

12. Tian, Z., Li, M., Qiu, M., Sun, Y., Shen, S.: Block-DEF: a secure digital evidence framework using blockchain. Inf. Sci. **491**, 151–165 (2019)

13. Pourvahab, M., Ekbatanifard, G.: Digital forensics architecture for evidence collection and provenance preservation in IaaS cloud environment using SDN and blockchain technology. IEEE Access **7**, 153349–153364 (2019)

14. Ateniese, G., et al.: Provable data possession at untrusted stores. In: Ning, P., De Capitani di Vimercati, S., Syverson, P.F. (eds.) Proceedings of the 2007 ACM Conference on Computer and Communications Security. CCS 2007, Alexandria, Virginia, USA, 28–31 October 2007, pp. 598–609. ACM (2007)

15. Guo, J., Yang, W., Lam, K.-Y., Yi, X.: Using blockchain to control access to cloud data. In: Guo, F., Huang, X., Yung, M. (eds.) Inscrypt 2018. LNCS, vol. 11449, pp. 274–288. Springer, Cham (2019). https://doi.org/10.1007/978-3-030-14234-6_15

16. Wang, C., Chen, S., Feng, Z., Jiang, Y., Xue, X.: Block chain-based data audit and access control mechanism in service collaboration. In: Bertino, E., Chang, C.K., Chen, P., Damiani, E., Goul, M., Oyama, K. (eds.) 2019 IEEE International Conference on Web Services. ICWS 2019, Milan, Italy, 8–13 July 2019, pp. 214–218. IEEE (2019)

17. Yang, C., Tan, L., Shi, N., Bolei, X., Cao, Y., Keping, Yu.: AuthPrivacyChain: a blockchain-based access control framework with privacy protection in cloud. IEEE Access **8**, 70604–70615 (2020)

18. Sohrabi, N., Yi, X., Tari, Z., Khalil, I.: BACC: blockchain-based access control for cloud data. In: Jayaraman, P.P., Georgakopoulos, D., Sellis, T.K., Forkan, A. (eds.) Proceedings of the Australasian Computer Science Week. ACSW 2020, Melbourne, VIC, Australia, 3–7 February 2020, pp. 10:1–10:10. ACM (2020)

19. Jemel, M., Serrhrouchni, A.: Decentralized access control mechanism with temporal dimension based on blockchain. In: Hussain, O., Jiang, L., Fei, X., Lan, C.-W., Chao, K.-M. (eds.) 14th IEEE International Conference on e-Business Engineering. ICEBE 2017, Shanghai, China, 4–6 November 2017, pp. 177–182. IEEE Computer Society (2017)

20. Bethencourt, J., Sahai, A., Waters, B.: Ciphertext-policy attribute-based encryption. In: 2007 IEEE Symposium on Security and Privacy (S&P 2007), Oakland, California, USA, 20–23 May 2007, pp. 321–334. IEEE Computer Society (2007)

21. Zhang, X., Poslad, S., Ma, Z.: Block-based access control for blockchain-based electronic medical records (EMRs) query in eHealth. In: IEEE Global Communications Conference, GLOBECOM 2018, Abu Dhabi, United Arab Emirates, 9–13 December 2018, pp. 1–7. IEEE (2018)

22. Waters, B.: Ciphertext-policy attribute-based encryption: an expressive, efficient, and provably secure realization. In: Catalano, D., Fazio, N., Gennaro, R., Nicolosi, A. (eds.) PKC 2011. LNCS, vol. 6571, pp. 53–70. Springer, Heidelberg (2011). https://doi.org/10.1007/978-3-642-19379-8_4
23. Zheng, L.J.: Research and design of authentication protocol in identity and location separation network (2014)

A Blockchain-Based Digital Copyright Protection System with Security and Efficiency

Zibin Xu, Lijun Wei, Jing Wu, and Chengnian Long[✉]

Department of Automation, Shanghai Jiao Tong University, Shanghai 200240, China
longcn@sjtu.edu.cn

Abstract. Today's digital copyright protection system is completely centralized and the confirmation and transaction of copyright depend entirely on a third party, which suffers from time-consumption, high cost and data isolation. In this paper, we propose a secure and efficient digital copyright protection system based on blockchain technology and IPFS that provides a whole process of copyright protection services including confirmation, registration, subscription, buying, tracing and querying. A series of encryption algorithms are adopted to ensure the security of the system and smart contracts are utilized to achieve automatic confirmation and transaction of copyright. Moreover, we present key aspects related to architectural design and interactions details between system components. In order to validate the proposed system, we evaluated the whole system in terms of function, performance and security aspects. Our test and analysis suggest that the proposed system can help to solve the problem caused by the current copyright protection system.

Keywords: Digital copyright · Blockchain · Smart contract · IPFS

1 Introduction

Copyright is used to describe the rights that creators have over their literary or artistic works including music, books, paintings, films, and so on. It plays an essential role in fostering innovation, promoting economic growth, and spurring social changes [1,19]. With the rapid development of digital technology, more and more works have been published on the internet, the right protection of original creators and content integrity assurance have gradually become a pressing issue that needs to be resolved.

However, the intangible nature of digital works, combined with the increasingly convenient and low-cost information dissemination poses a great challenge for preserving digital copyright in a centralized way. Firstly, numerous individual original creators such as musicians, film producers, and photographers experience a constant struggle in today's digital world because they couldn't get compensated fairly and even unable to afford litigation when a copyright conflict occurs.

K. Xu et al. (Eds.): CBCC 2020, CCIS 1305, pp. 34–49, 2021.
https://doi.org/10.1007/978-981-33-6478-3_3

This stems from the fact that the low efficiency and high cost relying on third parties when a digital work needs to be authorized, subscribed and transferred. Secondly, there is no designated way for creators to legitimize their ownership of the work prior to its publication because of the lack of any official document or timestamp proving which version of the work came first. Moreover, different areas have different work registration strategy and preserving digital copyright is yet to be settled at the international level since the data isolation problem.

In this paper, we use blockchain technology, combined with the Inter-Planetary File System (IPFS) [2] and smart contracts to provide a secure and efficient digital copyright protection system. IPFS is a peer-to-peer distrusted file system used for trusted, secure, and reliable storage in which if one node goes down, other nodes in the network can still serve needed files. Once the information is stored into the blockchain, it will permanently be stored in the network and cannot be modified or deleted. Considering that it is not practical to store all information directly in the blockchain owing to the storage burden of blockchain, the blockchain is responsible for recording the metadata of the content to provide strong and high-level reliability of determining ownership and IPFS is utilized to store all raw content data. Smart contracts could help streamline and automate copyright confirmation and transaction processes that diminish the need to have a third party. Creators can interact directly with those who want to subscribe or buy the content through smart contracts.

In our proposed system, original creators can obtain remuneration fairly according to different contributions to the work and they are able to set different subscription prices according to different purposes of consumers. Besides, they can autonomously determine whether the copyright is transferable and transfer price. Before a creator registers the content information on the blockchain network, content duplication detection should be performed to avoid involving the plagiarism problem. The detection is realized by duplication algorithms such as Simhash for text detection [3], image duplication detection algorithm [4]. The certification authority will authenticate the work that has passed the detection by digital algorithm ECDSA. Considering anyone who has access to the hash address of the file can access its content [2], the system uses the efficient symmetric encryption AES algorithm to prevent the content from being used maliciously and asymmetric encryption RSA to realize key exchange securely.

This paper focuses on illustrating how blockchain and IPFS can be used to provide a secure, credible, efficient digital copyright protection system. The main contributions of this paper can be summarized as follows:

- We propose a blockchain-based digital copyright protection system using smart contracts and IPFS that is highly decentralized, efficient, and reliable. Several cryptographic algorithms are used to guarantee the security of the system.
- We present details on system architecture, design, work flow and the interactions of the various participants in the system.
- We provide a complete implementation of the smart contract and the full code was made publicly at Github.

– We provide function test to validate the correct interaction of the various participants and performance test to evaluate the efficiency of the system, with security analysis for the system.

The remainder of the paper is organized as follows. Section 2 summarizes the related work that exists in the literature and compares them to ours. Section 3 presents our system architecture and design of cryptography. Section 4 evaluates the proposed system by function and performance test and analyze the security of the system. Section 5 concludes the paper.

2   Related Work

With the emerge of blockchain technology such as bitcoin [5], ethereum [6], researchers are paying more attention to build an efficient digital copyright protection system based on this technology in the recent era. In this section, we summarize some studies that utilize blockchain to solve existing intellectual property problems.

Zhao et al. in [7] designed an image network copyright transaction protection scheme based on blockchain technology and described a realization structure of copyright market transactions. This work used Bitcoin network where participants agree with each other through PoW consensus mechanism, which is inefficient and energy-consuming. Authors in [8] proposed an intellectual property protection system using IoT and blockchain technologies. IoT devices are used to collect some location and transportation environment data as evidence. This proposed system can process three types of intellectual property based on the Maker-IP platform. In [9], authors designed a blockchain-based intellectual-property protection model for microfilms, which provides different blockchains such as TBC, ABC, MBC for different functionalities. Information registered in this system can not be notified. However, the details of implementation were not given in these works.

Digital watermarking technology [10] is used in digital copyright protection by embedding some important hidden information in the digital works with high robustness. In [11], a design scheme of a copyright management system based on blockchain and watermarking is proposed. Blockchain is used to store watermark securely and provides timestamp authentication for multiple watermarks. IPFS and QR code are also be used to generate and store watermarked images without a centralized server. Authors in [12] presented a tamper-proof media transaction framework based on blockchain and watermarking technologies to prevent original digital works from being tampered in media production workflow. The hash of transaction histories information and original media content are contained in watermark information, which is used to historical transaction retrieval and tampered content identification.

Digital rights management (DRM) [13] is one of the technologies meant to prevent or allow access only in specific instances set by right holders. In paper [14], authors discussed 3D printing technology and described the use of DRM as the main factor for the successful transition to Additive Manufacturing methods.

Blochkchain technology is used to secure the authenticity of printing data and prevent unauthorized use of it. Zhang and Zhao in [15] proposed a blockchain-based decentralized DRM mechanism in which information regarding transaction and license is recorded on the blockchain and transparent to everyone. Transaction reliability and automatic issuance of licenses depend on smart contracts rather than centralized servers. The mechanism allows copyright holders to set prices for different content usage rules flexible. However, nodes of the network have to possess high computational power to perform key acquisitions. Ma et al. in [16] presented a digital rights management scheme using blockchain, which is called as DRMchain. Two separate blockchains are designed, one is to store the original content with its cipher summary, and the other stores the cipher summary of protected digital content. The solution achieved secure authentication, privacy protection, and use of multi signatures for usage control.

The above works are based on permissionless (public) blockchain in which virtually anyone can participate and every participant is anonymous. In such a network, the economic incentive is provided in order to mitigate the absence of trust and offset the cost of participating in a form of byzantine fault-tolerant consensus based on POW. In our scheme, a consortium blockchain-based copyright protection system is proposed, where actors perform under a governance model that yields a certain degree of trust. Participants can interact in a secure way without fully trust each other, which is more suitable for copyright protection than public blockchain.

3   System Architecture and Design

In this section, we present an overview of the proposed blockchain-based system for preserving digital copyright that utilizes smart contracts and IPFS. In addition, we implement the system based on a consortium blockchain in which only the authenticated users can join and validation is performed by only pre-selected nodes. It usually achieves higher performance and security compared with public blockchains. In order to avoid the heavy cost of storing content information on the blockchain network, the system stores all content information in an off-chain way (IPFS) and records the metadata of the content on the blockchain. It will not incur high storage overhead since we assume amount of metadata is much smaller than the raw data.

3.1   System Architecture

Figure 1 describes the system architecture showing different actors and entities that will interact with the smart contract and IPFS. The system architecture consists of three key system components: Consortium Blockchain Network, IPFS, Users and Trusted Authorities. The participants (or actors) can be summarized as follows:

- **Consortium Blockchain Network:** The consortium blockchain network is the core of our proposed scheme, which is made of authorized nodes (i.e., trusted authority). It is used to securely store the metadata of the content and transaction information for timestamp authentication and tracing purpose.

- **IPFS**: IPFS is the storage system that encrypted content will be upload to. IPFS creates a hash address of the file based on its content and the node ID when a file is added to the network. The content hash returned from IPFS will be recorded on the blockchain along with the smart contract, as a part of the metadata.

- **Users**: Users are divided into creators, subscribers, and buyers. Creators are the original owners of the content. Subscribers are people who want to get access to the content, for instance, listening to music, watching movies, or download pictures. Buyers are those who want to buy the copyright. These transactions among them are implemented by using smart contracts. Users can act as light nodes in the blockchain network, they generally don't take part in the process of consensus and store all the ledger data.

- **Trusted Authorities (TAs)**: TAs including Membership service provider (MSP), Certification Authority (CA), Regulator. MSP defines the rules that govern valid identities for this network so that users can get permission to participate in the blockchain network. CA is responsible for testing the work submitted by the creators through duplication detection smart contract and generating certificates for contents which have passed the detection. The regulator protects copyright information and handles copyright disputes. Generally, TAs perform as full nodes in the network since their powerful storage and computational capacity.

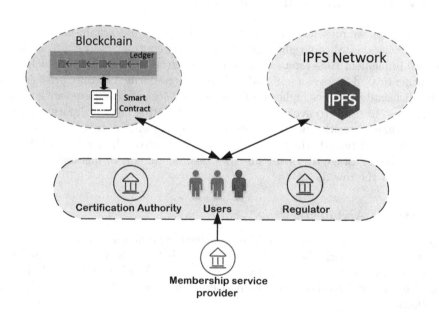

Fig. 1. System architecture.

It is worth noting that we assume the TAs is fully trusted. In the permissioned context, the participants are audited by MSP and are known to each other rather than being completely anonymous. Therefore, the risk of intentionally introducing malicious code through a smart contract is diminished and the guilty actor can be easily identified and punished by the regulator.

3.2 Cryptographic Techniques Used in the System

Symmetric-key cryptography is high-efficiency in providing security to the message (about 100–1000 times faster than asymmetric cryptography) but suffers from key distribution and management problems. In fact, Diffie-Hellman key exchange algorithm [17] provides a secure way that allows two parties to establish a shared cryptographic key over a public channel, but it is vulnerable to man-in-the-middle attacks since no identifying information is provided in the algorithm. In our system, we use symmetric encryption AES algorithm, combined with asymmetric encryption RSA algorithm to realize content protection and prevent the communication from being hijacked by attackers. And the ECSDA is used by CA for content authentication.

(1) Content Authentication

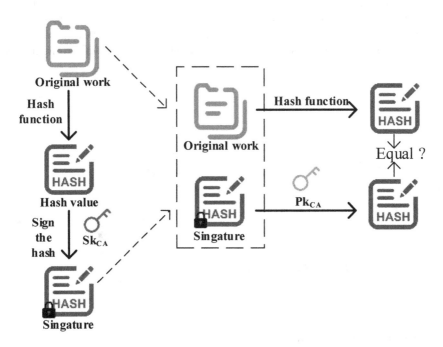

Fig. 2. The process of signing/verifying process of the digital signature.

Content authentication means the content has passed the duplication detection and be recognized the legitimacy, it is realized by digital signature which is only provided by CA. Once the original content passes the duplication detection, the CA will add the digital signature to the content using the secret key sk_{CA} as an official authentication, which means only the CA has the right to add the trusted signature. Users can verify the digital signature by the public key pk_{CA}. Figure 2 describes the signing/verifying process of the digital signature.

(2) Content Encryption and Key Exchange

Both blockchain and IPFS network is a transparent environment. Due to anyone who has the hash of content can get the content, encryption is necessary for the copyright owner to prevent the content from being freely used. The key to encrypt the content of the owner is also encrypted by the public key of the subscriber or buyer. The middle man is unable to do malicious behaviors since the public key is known to everyone. Figure 3 shows the whole process of content encryption and key exchange.

A represents the content owner, B represents the subscribers or buyers. Content owner encrypts the original work and digital signature form CA using the secret key sk_A. Once the content has been subscribed or bought, they need to decrypt the cipher content obtained from IPFS. The owner uses the public key of B pk_B to encrypt the secret key sk_A and send the data package to B. After receiving the data package, B can use his/her secret key sk_B to decrypt the encrypted key sk_A, and then use the key to get the content. Signature is a proof that the content has been passed the detection of CA, and B can verify the content through the signature by the content authentication method mentioned above.

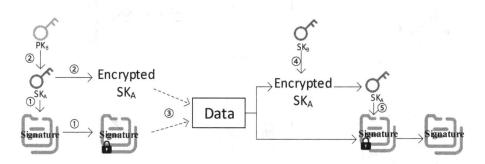

Fig. 3. Content encryption and key exchange.

3.3   Smart Contract Design

In this part, we introduce the smart contracts used in the proposed system. Table 1 shows the contract function and the corresponding permissions.

Table 1. Smart Contract.

Smart Contract	Function	Permission
$QueryUserInfo()$	Query user information	Person
$QueryContInfo()$	Query content information	All participants
$QueryAllUserInfo()$	Query all users information	TAs
$QueryAllContInfo()$	Query all contents information	All participants
$Submit()$	Submit metadata information of content	All participants
$Subscribe()$	Subscribe the content	All participants
$Buy()$	Buy the copyright of content	All participants

4   Implementation Details

Our solution was built on Hyperledger Fabric platform and the whole smart contract was implemented using Go programming language. The full code of our smart contract in Go language is made available at GitHub[1]. Figure 4 describes specific implementation details.

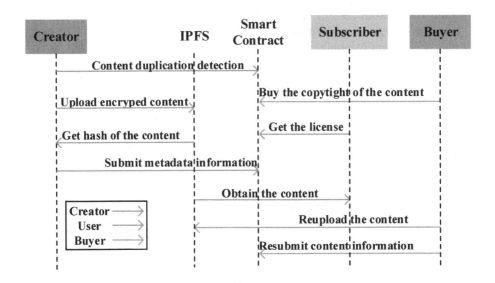

Fig. 4. The workfolw of the system.

(1) **Content Authentication.** Initially, CA creates the content duplication detection smart contract and signs the content that has passed the detection. Only contents that pass this verification can be subscribed or transaction. It is

---

[1] https://github.com/Xubin-source/Copyright-/blob/master/CP.go.

a key step to prevent plagiarized works from being uploaded to the blockchain. The process of signing/verifying as follows:

Step 1: CA randomly selects k and computes r as the temporary public key, where $H()$ is the hash function:

$$(x, y) = k \times G \tag{1}$$

$$r = x \bmod n (r \neq 0) \tag{2}$$

$$e = H(content) \tag{3}$$

Step 2: Then the CA computes s, and takes (r, s) as the signature information:

$$s = k^{-1}(e + r\, sk_{CA}) \bmod n (s \neq 0) \tag{4}$$

Step 3: When user receives the signature, then he or she verifies the signature as follows:

$$u_1 = s^{-1} \times e \bmod n \tag{5}$$

$$u_2 = s^{-1} \times r \bmod n \tag{6}$$

$$(x_p, y_p) = u_1 \times G + u_2 \times pk_{CA} \tag{7}$$

(2) Content Submission. After the content passes the detection smart contract, the content creator encrypts the digital content by the symmetric key S. The entire AES encryption/decryption process is as follows:

Step 1: Owners combine original content and digital signature of CA as the input data D of the encryption algorithm.

$$D = (content | DSA) \tag{8}$$

Step 2: The scheme calculates the cipher content C through the AES algorithm and the *Message Authentication Code* of input data using MAC function (HMAC-SHA-256), where v is a random number, and MAC is responsible for decryption check:

$$C = EN_{AES}(D, v, S) \tag{9}$$

$$MAC_{EN} = HMAC(D, S) \tag{10}$$

Then the content creator adds the cipher content C to the IPFS network, and he or she uploads the hash obtained from IPFS to the blockchain network as one of the parts of the metadata of the content information. The metadata information of the submitted content is shown in Fig. 5. The applicant is generally the primary creator of the content and has the greatest contribution to the work. Id is the unique identifier of the participants or the content. The contribution is used to realize a reasonable allocation of remuneration when the content has been subscribed or purchased. Subscription price and transfer price are set by creators. Subscription price can be set according to different purposes of subscribers. And the content can be set non-transferale. Creators can also upload the main content or core ideas to the blockchain network before the work is completed, to confirm the creation order in case there is a copyright conflict.

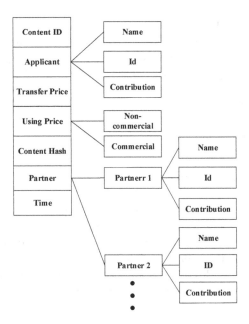

Fig. 5. The structure of meta data.

(3) Content Subscription. A subscriber can get permission to use the content by calling the *subscribe*() function. The subscription process will fail if the subscriber has no sufficient balance or input an incorrect parameter. After the function is successfully executed, the account status of both parties will change and the subscriber can get access to use the content and obtains the encrypted content through the content hash from IPFS.

(4) Copyright Transfer. Similar to subscribe content, the buyer call *Buy*() function to finish the transfer of copyright. Buy it would be failed to execute in the case of the original owner set the copyright is not transferable or the purchaser has no sufficient balance. Information on the content will be changed after successfully finish the transfer process. The updated contribution information depends on the purchase ratio of buyers. Except get access to the content, the new copyright owner(s) can do any operations with the content, including modification, re-encryption and re-upload it. Meanwhile, the original right owners will get fair remuneration by different contributions share.

(5) Signature Verification. Once users (subscribers or buyers) receives the cipher data and gets the key S, then decrypts the cipher data and calculates the MAC from the decrypted data as follows:

$$D_{de} = DE_{AES}(C, v, S) \qquad (11)$$

$$MAC_{DE} = HMAC(D, S) \qquad (12)$$

If the MAC of input data and MAC of the output is the same, the decryption is successful.

(6) Information Querying. The system provides $QueryInfo()$ contract to query the information about a user or a content with a unique identification, $QueryAllContInfo()$ to query all content information and $QueryAllUserInfo$ to query all users information. But these contract is not available for all the participants since calling these smart contract need different permissions. For users, they can query content information and their personal information including $<Name, Id, Account, SubscribedContent>$. CA and regulator have access to query all the information for better management.

5   Validation and Analysis

In this section, we implement our system on Hyperledger Fabric v1.4 which supports smart contracts called chaincodes and test all the functionalities that the system provides. We also test the performance of the system to evaluate whether the system that we proposed can meet the requirements of the actual application scenario. In addition, We provide a comparison of the digital signature algorithms and discuss the different usage scenarios of them and analyze the security of the whole system.

5.1   Function Test

In this part, we mainly focus on testing the correct interaction among participants in this system. For the purpose of testing, we classify subscription purposes as commercial and non-commercial, and the commercial price is set to 10 times the non-commercial price. It means that the copyright of the content is not transferable if the transfer price is set to NULL.

(1) Query Information. After running Hyperledger Fabric network, we initialized the system with two contents and eight users. Then we queried the users' information and retrieved related information of each upload content. Table 2 shows the information of participants and Table 3 shows the content information.

Table 2. Users information.

Name	Id	Account	Subscribed Content
A	000	100	cont1
A1	001	100	–
B	100	50	cont0
B1	101	100	cont0
B2	102	70	–
C	200	150	–
D	300	1000	–
E	400	1000	–

Table 3. Contents information.

Content Id	Applicant			UsingPrice	TransferPrice	Partner(s)			HashValue	Time
	Name	Id	Contribution			Name	Id	Contribution		
Cont0	A	000	50	20	500	A1	001	50	QmQU2gS4gZ7TpiTECjDUxdQFd 9bBBEWxDxPPfhLfYHVuei	2020-07-15 19:05:28
Cont1	B	100	50	50	-	B1	101	30	QmQU2gS4gZ7TpiTECjDUxd	2020-08-15
						B2	102	20	QFd9bBBEWxDxPPfhLfYHVuei	22:08:34

(2) Submit Content. We call the *Submit*() smart contract to submit content 2 to the network, which is created by C and D. Then we query the information of content 2 by its content ID through the *queryinfo* contract to ensure the content is recorded by blockchain correctly. The result is shown in Fig. 6.

```
"Content2":{
"Applicant":{"Name":"C","Id":"200","Con":"50"},
"Usingprice":"20",
"TransferPrice":"20",
"PartnerInfo":{"Name":"D","Id":"300","Con":"50"},
"Hashvalue":"QmZB8R7T5xvKJDUJ6pXtUym6frQx1r6bQPcwquR1rtGHL6",
"Time":"2020-08-16 10:06:51"}
```

Fig. 6. The information of content 2 of submitting it.

(3) Subscribe Content. C subscribes content 0 for non-commercial purpose by calling *subscribe*() smart contract. Creators A and A0 get remuneration according to their respective contribution. The personal information of A, A0, C is shown in Fig. 7.

```
{"Name":"A","Id":"000","Account":"101","Subscribed content":"cont1",
"Name":"A1","Id":"001","Account":"101","Subscribed content":"",
"Name":"C","Id":"200","Account":"148","Subscribed content":"cont0",
```

Fig. 7. Information of A, A0, C after subcribering content 0

(4) Copyright Transfer. We firstly try to buy the copyright of content 1 but it failed because it is set not transferable by original owners. After successfully buy the copyright, new applicant will re-encrypt the content using his/her Secret key and re-submit the information to the blockchain. Figure 8 shows the copyright information that new applicant re-submit and counterparty balance information after successfully finishing copyright purchase of content0 by D and E. The new contribution is equivalent to the investment proportion.

"Content0": {
"Applicant: {"Name":"D","Id":"300","Con":"50"},
"Usingprice":"5",
"TransferPrice":"",
"PartnerInfo":"Name":"E","Id":"400","Con":"50",
"Hashvalue":"Qm3f4036a1164d1ddbad5b3edf9022addb3e1961a54a99"
"Time":"2020-08-18 14:06:09}

{"Name":"A","Id":"000","Account":"351","Subscribed content":"",
"Name":"A1","Id":"001","Account":"351","Subscribed content":"",
"Name":"D","Id":"300","Account":"750","Subscribed content":"",
"Name":"E","Id":"400","Account":"750","Subscribed content":""}

Fig. 8. Information of content 0 and users

5.2   Performance Test

We conducted our experiments on ubuntu 18.4 version with an Intel Core i5 CPU at 2.7 GHz with 4 GB RAM with a 500 GB hard drive and the bandwidth is 10 Mbps. The system is initialized with 4 nodes, 2 organizations and 1 channel. We used Hyperledger Caliper benchmark tool to evaluate the transaction per second (TPS) and latency of the system. Figure 9 depicts the test results of performing different types of operations.

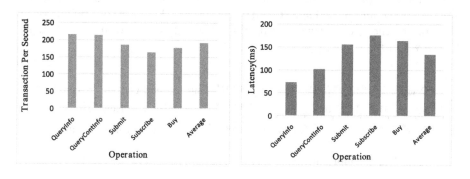

Fig. 9. Performance test results

The experimental results show that the performance of the system is much better than traditional public blockchain (4–5 TPS and 10min latency for Bitcoin, 30–40 TPS and 10–20 latency for Ethereum). Considering the highly concurrent transactions are not necessary is the practical application scenario of the system, the result is sufficient to satisfy the real scenario requirements. Actually, not all the nodes in the consortium blockchain will participate in the transaction processing, and many experiments have shown that there will be a great improvement in performance with better and higher bandwidth even with many nodes in the network [18].

5.3 Security Analysis

In this part, we analyze the security of the system by presenting several possible attack models. We are not concerned about how attackers launch different attacks but focus on how the system can defend the system against these possible attacks.

(1) Single point of failure. A single point of failure means that if a part of system fails, the entire system will stop working, which is undesirable in any system with high availability and reliability. Our system operates in a distributed way, it allows up to $1/2$ nodes fail (crash failure) in case of RAFT consensus and tolerates up to $1/3$ nodes fails(crash and Byzantine failure) in case of PBFT consensus.

(2) Sybil attack. In a peer-to-peer network, each node has a unique identity node id. In sybil attack, the attacker subverts the system of network service by creating a large number of pseudonymous identities and attempts to use them to gain a disproportionately large influence. In our scheme, all nodes that want to participant in the system must be authenticated by the MSP, nodes with false identities will not be recognized. Therefore, there is no sybil attack in the system.

(3) Man in the middle attack. A man-in-the-middle attack is a type of cyberattack where a malicious actor intercepts communications between two parties either to secretly eavesdrop or modify the communications between two parties. In our system, each participant has a public-secret key pair in which the public key is known to everyone hence middlemen is unable to forge or alert it, and even though attackers can intercept their public keys, none of them can calculate their private keys from this information because of the discrete logarithm problem.

6   Conclusion

In this paper, we present a solution that utilizes consortium blockchain, smart contracts, and IPFS to provide a secure, efficient, and trusted platform for digital copyright protection with high integrity and traceability. Blockchain is responsible for immutable timestamp authentication of the copyright and IPFS is used to store raw data of content. Smart contract automates copyright confirmation and transaction processes and ensures fair remuneration via different contributions. We utilize several cryptographic algorithms to realize content protection and key exchange. We also implement smart contracts and test the overall system functionalities and evaluate system performance. As future work, we aim to implement a system with better security and performance.

Acknowledgement. This work was supported in part by the National Natural Science Foundation of China under Grants 62073215, 61873166 and 61673275, in part by the Science and Technology Commission Shanghai Municipality under Grant 19511102102, and in part by the Shanghai Automotive Industry Technology Development Foundation under Grant 2008.

References

1. Mermer, J.E.: The impact of intellectual property in fostering innovation. Available at SSRN 3379331 (2018)
2. Benet, J.: IPFS-content addressed, versioned, P2P file system. arXiv preprint arXiv:1407.3561 (2014)
3. Manku, G.S., Jain, A., Das Sarma, A.: Detecting near-duplicates for web crawling. In: Proceedings of the 16th International Conference on World Wide Web, pp. 141–150 (2007). https://doi.org/10.1145/1242572.1242592
4. Ke, Y., Sukthankar, R., Huston, L., Ke, Y., Sukthankar, R.: Efficient near-duplicate detection and sub-image retrieval. In: ACM multimedia, vol. 4, p. 5. Citeseer (2004)
5. Nakamoto, S.: Bitcoin: A peer-to-peer electronic cash system. Technical report, Manubot (2019)
6. Wood, G., et al.: Ethereum: a secure decentralised generalised transaction ledger. Ethereum Proj. Yellow Pap. **151**(2014), 1–32 (2014)
7. Zhao, C., Liu, M., Yang, Y., Zhao, F., Chen, S.: Toward a blockchain based image network copyright transaction protection approach. In: Yang, C.-N., Peng, S.-L., Jain, L.C. (eds.) SICBS 2018. AISC, vol. 895, pp. 17–28. Springer, Cham (2020). https://doi.org/10.1007/978-3-030-16946-6_2
8. Lin, J., Long, W., Zhang, A., Chai, Y.: Using blockchain and IoT technologies to enhance intellectual property protection. In: Proceedings of the 4th International Conference on Crowd Science and Engineering, pp. 44–49 (2019)
9. Tsai, W.T., Feng, L., Zhang, H., You, Y., Wang, L., Zhong, Y.: Intellectual-property blockchain-based protection model for microfilms. In: 2017 IEEE Symposium on Service-Oriented System Engineering (SOSE), pp. 174–178. IEEE (2017)
10. Allayla, H.F.H.: Copyright protection using digital watermarking. Master's thesis, Çankaya Üniversitesi (2017)
11. Meng, Z., Morizumi, T., Miyata, S., Kinoshita, H.: Design scheme of copyright management system based on digital watermarking and blockchain. In: 2018 IEEE 42nd Annual Computer Software and Applications Conference (COMPSAC), vol. 2, pp. 359–364. IEEE (2018)
12. Bhowmik, D., Feng, T.: The multimedia blockchain: a distributed and tamper-proof media transaction framework. In: 2017 22nd International Conference on Digital Signal Processing (DSP), pp. 1–5. IEEE (2017)
13. Rosenblatt, B., Trippe, B., Mooney, S., et al.: Digital rights management, New York (2002)
14. Holland, M., Nigischer, C., Stjepandic, J.: Copyright protection in additive manufacturing with blockchain approach. Transdiscipl. Eng. Parad. Shift **5**, 914–921 (2017)
15. Zhang, Z., Zhao, L.: A design of digital rights management mechanism based on blockchain technology. In: Chen, S., Wang, H., Zhang, L.-J. (eds.) ICBC 2018. LNCS, vol. 10974, pp. 32–46. Springer, Cham (2018). https://doi.org/10.1007/978-3-319-94478-4_3

16. Ma, Z., Jiang, M., Gao, H., Wang, Z.: Blockchain for digital rights management. Future Gener. Comput. Syst. **89**, 746–764 (2018). https://doi.org/10.1016/j.future.2018.07.029

17. Diffie, W., Hellman, M.: New directions in cryptography. IEEE Trans. Inf. Theory **22**(6), 644–654 (1976). https://doi.org/10.1109/TIT.1976.1055638

18. Liu, Y., Qian, K., Yu, J., Wang, K., He, L.: Effective scaling of blockchain beyond consensus innovations and Moore's law. arXiv preprint arXiv:2001.01865 (2020)

19. Park, W.G., Ginarte, J.C.: Intellectual property rights and economic growth. Contemp. Econ. Policy **15**(3), 51–61 (1997). https://doi.org/10.1111/j.1465-7287.1997.tb00477.x

Multi-core and SIMD Architecture Based Implementation on SHA-256 of Blockchain

Xing Fan and Baoning Niu$^{(\boxtimes)}$

School of Information and Computer, Taiyuan University of Technology,
Jinzhong 030600, China
niubaoning@tyut.edu.cn

Abstract. SHA-256 is a completely unpredictable pseudorandom function which generates unique output for a given input ensuring data authenticity and non-repudiation. It is the cornerstone for imparting security and privacy into Blockchain and its efficiency of calculation decides the performance of Blockchain. In this paper, we propose two novel methods to accelerate the calculation of SHA-256 in different situations. To eliminate the useless operations, we present pre-expanded padding blocks and hard coded into the software. On this basis, for a single message containing multiple 512-bit message blocks, we propose Interleaved Multi-Vectorizing Message Scheduling (IMV-MS) to optimize the message schedule stage of SHA-256, which utilize the interleaved multi-vectorizing (IMV) to combine single instruction multiple data (SIMD) vectorization with SHA-256. It splits a vectorized program into multiple states, then it interleaves the execution of vectorized states from those running instances which can make full use of the data parallelism in SIMD. On the other hand, in the situation where we hash several messages simultaneously, we propose the modified SHA-256 which employs SIMD instructions and thread-level parallelism technology together to realize parallel optimization on SHA-256. As experimental results show, IMV-MS and the proposed SHA-256 achieves up to 6.36X, 60.38X better performance compared with the pure SIMD vectorization and the pure scalar implementation, respectively.

Keywords: SHA-256 · Blockchain · SIMD

1 Introduction

Blockchain is one of the most noteworthy technologies in recent years. The computation of Blockchain features the frequent use of hash operations. Hash functions and digital signatures, the crypto-primitives behind Blockchain technology, depend on hash operations. Blocks are chained using hash to keep immutability, while data are signed digitally to ensure authenticity.

One of the mostly used hash operations is SHA-256 (Secure Hash Algorithm-256) [1], a hash algorithm turning an arbitrarily-large amount of data into a fixed-length hash value, and belonging to a family of cryptographic hash functions known as SHA-2. With strong collision resistance, unidirectional irreversible and puzzle-friendliness, SHA-256

© Springer Nature Singapore Pte Ltd. 2021
K. Xu et al. (Eds.): CBCC 2020, CCIS 1305, pp. 50–65, 2021.
https://doi.org/10.1007/978-981-33-6478-3_4

has been widely used as the encryption primitive in several different components of Blockchain applications, such as Bitcoin [2] and Hyperledger Fabric [3]. Bitcoin uses the double SHA-256 hashing algorithm, i.e. $SHA-256(SHA-256(x))$, in ① the creation of the Bitcoin address, the public key hash and the checksum; ② the construction of Merkle tree, a binary tree of hashes used for organizing transactions and verifying transactions in Simplified Payment Verification (SPV); and ③ mining blocks according to the Proof of Work (PoW) consensus mechanism. In Hyperledger Fabric, SHA-256 servers as a core hash function of Blockchain Cryptographic Service Provider (BCCSP), and used in ① certifying trust authorities, such as root certificate, manager certificate, TLS certificate and so on; and ② the construction of Merkle tree. Although Ethereum [4] employs Keccak256 of SHA-3 instead of SHA-256, it is reported that in the upcoming release of Ethereum 2.0, Keccak256 algorithm will be abandoned in favor of SHA-256 algorithm to achieve standardization and improve interoperability with most existing and future Blockchain applications [5]. In a word, SHA-256 plays an increasingly important role in Blockchain.

SHA-256 is calculated in three stages. In the pre-processing stage, the initial message is appended with a bit of "1", k bits of "0" and 64 bits of the length identifier such that the total bit length can be right divided by 512 by assigning an appropriate value to k. The augmented message is then divided into message blocks with the fixed length of 512 bits. Eight 32-bit state vectors are set, and named as $A, B, C, D, E, F, G, and H$. During the message schedule stage, each message block is divided into 16 sub-blocks with the fixed length of 32 bits, which is then expanded to 64 sub-blocks using the equations (see Sect. 2). At last, the compression stage consists of 64 "rounds", which takes as inputs the eight state vectors, the corresponding sub-blocks, and a round-specific constant. After the calculation of the 64 rounds, the result is added to the original state vector to produce the new state vector. If the input consists of multiple blocks, this process is repeated for each block.

There exist three optimization opportunities in the calculation process of SHA-256. First, the messages to be processed by SHA-256 are almost the result of SHA-256, with a bit length of 256, except hashing the original transaction to produce the transaction hash. According to the use of SHA-256 in Blockchain, it always organized as $SHA-256(h_1||h_2)$, where both h_1 and h_2 are 256 bits, therefore the concatenated message $h_1||h_2$ is 512 bits. This means those messages need to be appended with the same 512 bits message block in the pre-processing stage which take the same operations in the message schedule stage and produce the same result. Taking the observations into account, the padding and message schedule operations can process once and use the result multiple times, or simply hard-coded. Second, for a given message such as the smart contract or the transaction data which contains several 512-bit message blocks, the canonical methods [1–3] are to process them one by one, or in a serialized sequence. Nevertheless, the message scheduling depends only on the message, and is independent of the intermediate values of the computed digest. This property allows for processing multiple message schedules in parallel. At last, there are frequent scenarios where multiple SHA-256 calculations of independent messages are needed, such as the construction of Merkle tree, the calculation of the block hash, or the verification of transactions. The state-of-the-art algorithms [1–3] process them in serialization without take the chance of parallel processing.

The first opportunity can be addressed by hard-coding the invariants into algorithms. Next, SHA-256 operation basically is a bit operation, which provides the calculation of SHA-256 with the opportunity to conduct data-level parallelism (DLP). Finally, for the scenarios where multiple SHA-256 calculations of independent messages are needed, the combination of DLP with thread-level parallelism (TLP) could improve the performance of software cryptographic.

Based on the discussions above, we argue that the efficiency of SHA-256 calculation, the most frequently used calculation in Blockchain, can be significantly improved by exploiting the properties of Blockchain data, and two parallel mechanisms, DLP and TLP. To turn the above-mentioned opportunities into realities, this paper proposes a highly efficient SHA-256 algorithm for Blockchain and claims the following contributions.

- Based on the analysis of Blockchain data characteristics, we find that the contents of the last message block are constant in most cases, so that the padding and message schedule operations can simply hard-coded into the algorithm to save the computing resources.
- We propose a method called IMV Message Scheduling (IMV-MS) for the single message to perfectly combine SIMD [14] vectorization and prefetching.
- We develop to calculate multiple messages in parallel under the combination of DLP with TLP to improve the performance of software cryptographic.

The rest of the paper is organized as follows. Section 2 describes related work. Section 3 analyzes how to optimize SHA-256 calculations as well as take full use of SIMD and multi-core architecture. Section 4 demonstrates our experimental evaluation. Finally, we conclude this paper in Sect. 5.

2   Related Work

An Overview of SHA-256 Algorithm. The basic computation for SHA-256 takes a block of input data that is 512 bits and a state vector that is 256 bits in size, and it produces a modified state vector. SHA-256 can be conveniently divided into three distinct operations as follows:

In pre-processing stage, we pad the message to make it a multiple of 512 bits, that is, assume the length of the message is l bits, the padding logic is such that it appends a bit "1" at the end of the actual message which is then followed by k number of "0" bits. Here, k satisfied that $(l + 1 + k) mod 512 = 448$, at the end of the message is the length information about this message which is 64 bits. Secondly, parse the newly message into l message blocks which contain 512-bit, and then set the eight 32-bit default state vector as A, B, C, D, E, F, G, H.

During the message scheduler stage, we take the first 512-bit message block and divide it into 16 32-bit sub-blocks, and then the 16 sub-blocks drive 64 sub-blocks for every round are labelled as W_t, $t \in [0, 63]$ and they are calculated as follows:

$$\sigma_0(x) = (x \ggg 7) \oplus (x \ggg 18) \oplus (x \gg 3) \tag{1}$$

$$\sigma_1(x) = (x \ggg 17) \oplus (x \ggg 19) \oplus (x \gg 10) \tag{2}$$

$$W_t = M_t (0 \le t \le 15) \tag{3}$$

$$W_t = \sigma_0(W_{t-15}) + \sigma_1(W_{t-2}) + W_{t-7} + W_{t-16} (16 \le t \le 63) \tag{4}$$

Compression stage performs the actual hashing operation and is the main operation of SHA-256. The SHA-256 algorithm consists mainly of a loop, as shown in Fig. 1. In each step, the 8 intermediate values are updated, and after 64 iterations, a result is generated by cascading them together. Details of the whole algorithm can be found in [1].

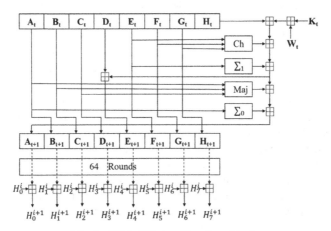

Fig. 1. SHA-256 algorithm for a block.

Optimizing SHA-256 Calculations. Optimizations [6] target towards the double SHA-256 hashing algorithm specific to the Bitcoin mining protocol, which take advantage of the fixed or predictable nature of the input stream of data in Bitcoin mining and various shortcuts to achieve the same computational results as off-the-shelf SHA-256. However, this method does not make full use of the existing computing resource and the optimization involve in ten aspects which is too tedious to implement.

SHA-256 is a standard hash thus optimizations mostly focus on the instructions or hardware. In this paper, aimed at the concatenated input messages are 512-bit, thus the content of the padding message block remains same, we propose to precompute its pre-processing and message schedule stages to save the useless computation efficiency.

Optimizing SHA-256 via Hardware. For the generic SHA-256, researchers [7, 8] propose utilizing the vector processor instructions (SIMD) to improve the overall algorithm's performance. Nevertheless this optimization has two shortcomings: ① this method only focus on the message scheduling phase which not make full use of the algorithm features to parallel; ② due to the time limit, the SIMD instruction of the paper is restricted to Advanced Vector eXtensions (AVX) which could extend to AVX2, AVX512 or other thread-level parallelism. Intel develop SHA extensions [9] architecture processors to support SHA-1 and SHA-256. But as of the time of this posting, the SHA extensions remain restricted to a very particular subset of Intel's offerings, including Pentium J4205, N4200 and the Celeron J3455 series.

In order to optimize SHA-256 operations, researchers propose to utilize dedicated hardware implementations. McEvoy et al. [10] employ Carry Save Adders (CSAs) to reduce the most complicated calculation of the working variable A for each round of the compression function by separating the sum and the carry paths. Unrolled architectures [11] reduce the number of clock cycles required to perform the SHA-256 hash computation by implementing multiple rounds of the SHA-256 compression function using combinational logic. This architecture help improves the throughput by optimizing the data dependencies involved in the message compression function. However, unrolling the SHA-256 core architecture comes at the cost of a decrease in the clock frequency and an increase in the area complexity. These optimizations are focus on the hardware implementations and optimizations of SHA-256 which is not well suited into the Blockchain applications.

Rather than the general SHA-256, the promise of a reward—miner bonus is a motivator for hardware acceleration which induces a wide field of SHA-256 hardware acceleration research. In Bitcoin system, the hardware evolved from CPUs to GPUs to FPGA to ASICs [12]. The methods [13] of performing Bitcoin mining on custom and non-custom hardware are discussed. In the non-custom hardware, the author investigates SHA-256 computations on CPU via the SSE2 instruction set and GPU via CUDA/OpenCL. With regard the custom hardware the author presents ASIC and FPGA miner. However, this paper merely focuses on the hardware acceleration which ignores using fast software implementations on general-purpose devices.

The literature has so far mainly concentrated on the new hardware, while the computing power of SIMD instructions, CPU and the characteristics of SHA-256 algorithm are underestimated or even ignored. In our study, we develop two novelty parallelism method for different situations that utilize SIMD instructions and multi-core architecture for general-purpose devices.

3   SHA-256 Optimizations in Blockchain

In this section we focus on two different situations in Blockchain: ① a single message which contains multiple message blocks with fixed length (512-bit); ② hash several messages for serialization. To begin with, we analyze SHA-256 operation pattern in Blockchain and then propose to utilize pre-expanded padding block in Sect. 3.1. To make full use of SIMD architecture to improve current implementation of SHA-256 algorithm for a single message, we develop IMV-MS which parallelize within a thread on several message blocks at the same time to speed up hash performance in Sect. 3.2. What's more, in Sect. 3.3 we describe a method for efficiently hashing multiple messages by parallelizing the computations and using multi-core SIMD architectures.

3.1 Utilize Pre-expanded Padding Block

It's worth noting that Blockchain utilizes SHA-256 as the basic hash function which means the data hash are 256 bits in length. So that during the hash calculations, such as the construction of Merkle tree and block hash, it always organized as $SHA-256(h_1 \| h_2)$, i.e. concatenate the two hash h_1, h_2 as a new message h and then perform the hash operation on it. In this section we focus on the fact that the length of the input variable never changes, so that we can take advantage of this nature to eliminate the superfluous operations.

For any hash values h_1, h_2, according to the pre-processing stage, the message need to padding "1" as an identifier, additional "0" and message length as described in Sect. 2. The input of h contains 512 bits of the message, followed by the identifier "1", then $k = 2 * 512 - (512 + 1 + 64) = 447$ bits for "0" and the length information is 64 bits which is marked as 0x00000200 in hex for 512 at last. Based on the above analysis, we can draw a conclusion that the values of the last message block contained in the inputs for h along with the round in which they enter the message compression algorithm (Table 1):

Table 1. $M_t (0 \leq t \leq 15)$ for each round of h in 2nd block.

Round	M_t	Description
0	0x80000000	"1" + Padding
1–13	0x00000000	Padding
14	0x00000000	Length
15	0x00000200	Length

As we know, the purpose of the pre-processing phase is to ensure the pending block are equal to 512 bits and identify the length of message. We can conclude that if the length of the hashed message is an integer multiple of the block size, i.e. 512-bit, the padding block can be pre-expanded. Thus, we can take advantage of this feature to simplify the hash operations, that is, use the pre-expanded padding block, so that we can eliminate the pre-processing as well as the message schedule phase. This optimization is useful for applications involves the construction of Merkle tree, block hash and so on, because the padding blocks for the relevant sizes can be pre-expanded.

3.2 Single-Core SIMD Implementation

In this section, we focus on how SIMD parallel computation model can improve software cryptographic performance. The SIMD [14] model speeds up the software performance by allowing the same operation to be carried out on multiple data elements in parallel. Instead, the conventional scalar execution model, which is called single instruction single data (SISD) deals only with one pair of data at a time. This architecture can be built easily by increasing the width of the data-path. Most of the current general-purpose computers employ SIMD architectures. AltiVec extension to PowerPC, Intel's MultiMedia eXtensions technology (MMX), AVX, AVX2 and AVX512, Sun's VIS and 3DNow! of AMD are examples of currently used SIMD technologies. We choose Intel Architecture as the base SIMD platform since it is the most widely used architecture.

Although SIMD instructions have the potential to speed-up SHA-256 algorithm, there exists one mismatch with SIMD model is that if the data layout does not match the SIMD requirements, SIMD instructions may not be used or data rearrangement code is necessary. Fortunately, SHA-256 uses 32-bit words. We utilize parameter N to describe the number of sub-blocks that fit into a given SIMD register:

$$N = \frac{l_{SIMD}}{l_{sub-block}}$$

the messages are divided into sub-blocks, $l_{sub-block} = 32$ bits. For the AVX architecture that supports $l_{SIMD} = 128$ bits registers, therefore $N = 4$. Similarly, for AVX2, AVX512 architectures where $l_{SIMD} = 256$ bits, 512 bits, thus $N = 8, 16$, respectively.

Message scheduler stage consumes ~27% of SHA-256 operations [7]. Obviously, optimizing the message scheduling in hash algorithms can have a significant effect on the overall performance. To speed up hashing on a message, we have to combine same operations of different rounds and use SIMD instructions to perform these operations at a time. In order to combine the same operation of two consecutive rounds, we must know the values that will be used in the next round while we are processing the round before. If we know these values in advance, we can successfully convert these operations into one SIMD instruction.

According to the message scheduler stage, the first 16 message sub-blocks are available immediately (they consist of the actual input sub-blocks). So, we compute W_{16} at first with N lanes at a time in the best case. In the traditional manner, we compute the message block in sequence which need the corresponding σ_0, σ_1 to get W_t finally which is shown in the first panel of Fig. 2.

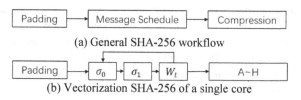

(a) General SHA-256 workflow

(b) Vectorization SHA-256 of a single core

Fig. 2. A pipeline example of general SHA-256 and vectorization SHA-256.

To facilitate our description, the execution pattern is shown in Fig. 3(a) under AVX2 architecture, denoted as Directly Vectorized Message Scheduling (DV-MS) where $N = 8$, $W_j^i(0 \le j \le 63)$ means j^{th} sub-block of ith message block. At first, lanes $L_0 - L_7$

repeat the σ_0, σ_1 and W_t operations as illustrated in formula (1) (2) (4). From formula (1) we obtain that σ_0 only depend on $\sigma_0(W_{t-15})$, so that we can compute it 8 at a time. Unfortunately, this does not extend to σ_1 since it relies on $\sigma_1(W_{t-2})$, so that the sub-expression needs to compute it 2 at a time which results to W_t have the same state as sub-expression σ_1. That is, we do one set of calculations to compute $\left\{\sigma_1\left(W_{14}^0\right), \sigma_1\left(W_{15}^0\right)\right\}$ and then we can get $\left\{W_{16}^0, W_{17}^0\right\}$. It is worth noting that such interleaving in the three expressions leads to many bubbles, i.e., the empty vector lanes, denoting inactive processing. For example, in Fig. 3(a), there are six out of inactive lanes are empty due to the restriction of function σ_1 and W_t in a vectorization instruction, so that we need 9 vectorized computations in total to get the 8 sub-blocks $\left\{W_{16}^0, W_{17}^0, \ldots, W_{23}^0\right\}$. Such inactive lanes result from the differences in data dependence of functions which would underutilizes the data parallelism provided by SIMD as well as making full use of memory level parallelism.

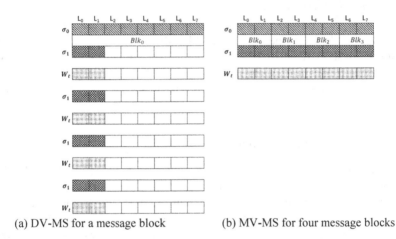

(a) DV-MS for a message block   (b) MV-MS for four message blocks

Fig. 3. Execution workflow of two interleaved approaches in message schedule.

In order to fully use SIMD vectorization, we propose to utilize interleaved multi-vectorizing (IMV) [15] to perfectly combine SIMD vectorization which called IMV Message Scheduling (IMV-MS). IMV splits a vectorized program into multiple states wherever the program meets the control flow divergence or immediate memory accesses, then it interleaves the execution of vectorized states from those running instances as shown in Fig. 2(b).

In contrast to DV-MS, a vectorized program is split into a series of states. In such a way, a group of interleaved running instances are suspended and resumed in turn, and each running instance has its own running contexts. The execution flow is shown in Fig. 3(b), where the workloads are the same as those in Fig. 3(a). In order to utilize all available lanes, we reorganize the two consecutive sub-blocks as a group and then compute the four message blocks at the same time in one operation. In this way, all new inactive vector lanes are filled with new sub-blocks of subsequent message blocks. In consequence, there are no bubbles in Fig. 3(b) compared to Fig. 3(a) which would make full use of SIMD resource. The alteration of SHA-256 message schedule lead to a more efficient workload, it needs $\frac{64-16}{2} * 3 = 72$ rounds for 4 message blocks.

Accordingly, in DV-MS, for 4 message blocks, we need $\left(\frac{64-16}{8} + \frac{64-16}{2} * 2\right) * 4 = 216$ rounds in total. Considered the equations with the general coefficients, we can obtain that we need

$$\left(\frac{64-16}{N} + \frac{64-16}{2} * 2\right) * \frac{N}{2} = 24(N+1) \tag{5}$$

rounds for N lanes of a register.

To further compare the cost of operations during message schedule between DV-MS and IMV-MS, we measure the lanes utilization factor by $f = \frac{l_{theory}}{l_{reality}}$, where l_{theory} means that the number of lanes needed for message schedule, whereas $l_{reality}$ denoted the number of rounds in practical. For the previous method, $f_{DV-MS} = \frac{48*3*4}{6*9*8*4} = 33.3\%$, whereas $f_{IMV-MS} = \frac{72*8}{6*9*8*4} = 100\%$. Combined with formula (5), we can draw a conclusion that as long as $24(N+1) > 72$, that is, $N > 2$, IMV-MS is more efficient than the former one obviously. In short, it can make full use of the data parallelism provided by SIMD. Take the various SIMD instructions into consideration, the performance advantage of this register utilization is more significance with the development of SIMD instruction set.

3.3 Multi-core SIMD Implementation

In the previous section, we improve the performance of SHA-256 with an algorithm that parallelizes the message schedule on SIMD architectures for a single message. In this section, we employ both thread-level parallelism (TLP) and data-level parallelism (DLP) architecture together to investigate the possibility of accelerating SHA-256 for some scenarios that hash a number (k) of independent messages simultaneously, to produce k different digests. Such workloads appear, for example, during the construction of Merkle tree or the transaction verification process, where the user checks the validity of the transaction through the Merkle branch. Another situation that involves hashing of multiple independent messages is orderer nodes of Hyperledger or miners of Bitcoin hash the initial transaction or block messages into the corresponding hash values.

Different to message schedule phase, the compression stage needs to be processed in a serial manner. That is, one cannot perform the calculations for round i, until the calculations for round $i - 1$ are completed.

Based on the above, the ways of SHA-256 computation in Blockchain for a message block is structured in this way: the message scheduling is done with IMV-MS, whereas the compression expressions are done with scalar instructions. These process loop through two code sequences: the message scheduling and the compression rounds as shown below. In particular, the first 16 sub-blocks are available immediately (they consist of the actual input message). Considered there are 8 lanes (AVX2 by default) in total, so we can compute 4 sub-blocks which regard as a group at a time as in Sect. 3.2, while the first 16 rounds are being computed, the message schedule $W_t(16 \leq t \leq 31)$ can be computed (Table 2).

Table 2. SHA-256 message scheduling and compression workflow.

Scalar implementation	SIMD implementation
Compress rounds ($0 \leq t \leq 15$)	Message schedule $W_t(16 \leq t \leq 31)$
Compress rounds ($16 \leq t \leq 31$)	Message schedule $W_t(32 \leq t \leq 47)$
Compress rounds ($32 \leq t \leq 47$)	Message schedule $W_t(48 \leq t \leq 63)$
Compress rounds ($48 \leq t \leq 63$)	

However, this workflow could not make full use of thread-level parallelism (TLP) with multi-core and data-level parallelism (DLP) architecture with SIMD together for the reason that such workflow still exists serial operations. Thus, we induce IMV-MS into both message schedule and compression stage of SHA-256, thus we regard a core as a unit and process N messages simultaneously. In other words, for a n-core processor, it can process $N * n$ messages simultaneously.

One further optimization is we find that in each compression operations, six (B, C, D, F, G, H) out of the eight $(A \sim H)$ state variables are shifted to the next state variable, so that we propose to rename the virtual registers (symbols) to affect this "shift" rather than do these using *mov* instructions. Thus, each round effectively rotates the set of state register names by one place. By doing r rounds which is a multiple of 8, the names have rotated back to their starting values, so no register moves are needed before looping.

4 Evaluation

In this section, we present a thorough evaluation of our proposed parallelization approaches on three different host processors. At first, in Sect. 4.1 we describe the compilation options and then show the target processor specifications in detail. Then we present and evaluate our experimental results on the different processor platforms as illustrated in Sect. 4.2.

4.1 Platform and Experimental Setup

The experiments were carried out on three processors: Intel® Core™ i7-3770, AMD Ryzen™ 7 2700X, Intel® Xeon® Bronze 3106, the hardware specifications of them are listed below (Table 3).

We take the SHA-256 which utilize in Bitcoin and Hyperledger as an evaluation criterion, denoted as General. Because of the different processors, the same SHA-256 algorithm may have various performance, thus we conduct the General one on three processors as the baseline. Here $N = 4, 8, 16$ represent the AVX ($l_{SIMD} = 128$), AVX2 ($l_{SIMD} = 256$) and AVX512 ($l_{SIMD} = 512$) instructions respectively. The performance is measured in MB/s. Here we define the average speed-up ratio as $S_{a/b} = \frac{v_a}{v_b}$ means the execution performance of a is $S_{a/b}$ times that of b.

Table 3. Details of hardware configuration.

CPU	SIMD instructions	Cores
Intel® Core™ i7-3770	AVX	4
AMD Ryzen™ 7 2700X	AVX, AVX2, SHA	8
Intel® Xeon® Bronze 3106	AVX, AVX2, AVX512	6

Since the Hyperledger is a permissioned Blockchain, its data are not available, thus we select Bitcoin data as the experimental data. To minimize the effect of background tasks running on the system, each experiment was repeated five times, and the minimum result was recorded.

To measure the performance of hashing data that resides in different cache levels the experiments are conducted on a machine with Intel® Core™ i7-3770K CPU that the general-purpose computer for definiteness and without loss of generality. Each core has independent L1 cache (L1 D-Cache 32 KB; L1 I-Cache 32 KB) and L2 cache (256 KB). 4 cores share L3 Cache (8 MB). All caches have 64-byte line size as default. The dataset is the transaction hash of equal size, where each block has $128item * 256bit = 4\,KB$ (Table 4).

Table 4. List of datasets.

No.	Cache level	Data volume (Items)	Block num.
1	L1	512	4
2	L2	8192	64
3	L3	61440	480
4	Main Memory	1024000	8000

4.2 Performance Evaluation

Utilize Pre-expanded Padding Block. To evaluate the benefit for hard coded the padding block for the single message which contains several message blocks, we carry an experiment on Intel® Core™ i7-3770, which is shown in Fig. 4. The data is the results of multi concatenated transaction hash value (256 bits) to fulfill different message lengths, each one has 1M pieces of data, all the data can fit into memory.

Figure 4 demonstrates the benefit of pre-expanding the last block which only contains padding and length messages for the length of the original concatenate message is a multiple of 512. The performance of SHA-256 with pre-expanded padding block is better than the generic SHA-256 in all cases. In general, the length of the original concatenate message is 512 bits (64 bytes), which means there are only 2 calls to the compression

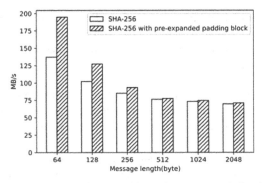

Fig. 4. Performance of SHA-256 with and without the pre-expanded padding optimization.

function (i.e., only two blocks are processed), thus it can achieve 1.42 times the speed of the general one. Such optimization is very useful for applications that hash many short message blocks of fixed lengths.

Single-core SIMD Implementation. For profiling the performance of the IMV-MS, we compare the resulting performance to DV-MS implementations that hash the same amount of data. The dataset is the original transaction data with diverse length. From the figure below, we can conclude that ① for the shorter message has a better performance compared to the longer one which is due to the IMV-MS only aim at message schedule phase, so that the shorter message need less additional compression operations accordingly. ② Because IMV-MS only for the single message, thus it executes serial compression operations which is why its performance is slightly less than the letter experiment results. ③ For further compare the relationship between the SIMD instructions and the performance, the right vertical axis describes the speed ratio. For AVX, it supports 128 bits, $N = \frac{128}{32} = 4$, we choose two sub-blocks as a group, thus it achieves 1.96X speeds than DV-MS. Accordingly, AVX512 supports 512 bits, $N = \frac{512}{32} = 16$, thus it achieves 1.95X, 2.84X, 4.24X and 6.36X performance compared to DV-MS (Fig. 5).

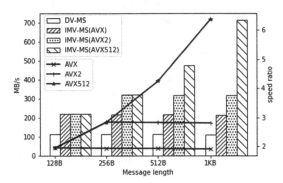

Fig. 5. Performance of IMV-MS on Intel® Xeon® Bronze 3106 with various message length.

Multi-core SIMD Implementation on Various Processors. To asses our proposed algorithm, we conduct a research on three processors on their supported SIMD instructions. The dataset is the original transaction data with diverse length, 1 M items in total, all the data can fit into memory.

Figure 6 shows the experimental results with different parallelism techniques on three different processors. Under the DLP model, the peak parallelism is N, whereas under the combination of DLP and TLP model, the peak parallelism can be calculated as $N * n$ in theory.

As for Intel® Core™ i7-3770, it only support AVX instruction set, the $S_{AVX/General}$ is approximately 3.17 and fluctuates in the tiny range. This value is smaller than the naively expected maximum value 4 for two reasons. One is the needed overhead for SIMD lanes schedule. Another one is that there are still some sequential operations that cannot be vectorized, such as data padding and communication. Similarly, $S_{AVX-2Core/General}$, $S_{AVX-4Core/General}$ reaches a maximum of 5.38, 8.61 respectively when n equals to 2 and 4.

Since AMD Ryzen™ 7 2700X supports SHA extensions, thus we select it as an experimental platform. In addition, it also supports AVX and AVX2. From Fig. 6(b), same as the performance in Intel® Core™ i7-3770, both $S_{AVX/General} \approx 3.37$ and $S_{AVX2/General} \approx 5.73$ tend to be constant. However, the speedup value $S_{AVX-General}$ is higher than the previous one which may due to the different CPU architectures. Obviously, AMD Ryzen™ 7 2700X is advanced in this aspect. Meanwhile, although AVX2 and AVX achieve better performance than the general algorithm, the SHA extensions obtains the best performance than others, where $S_{AVX-General} \approx 17.67$, the peak speed is 1979.00 MB/s. However, there are only a few series processors support SHA extensions when the which are not universally suitable for all platforms and users. With the combine of DLP and TLP, the performance is higher than SHA extensions which reaches 3798.55 MB/s at best when $n = 8$, where $S_{AVX2-8Core/General} \approx 2$.

In the third processor, the speed under AVX, AVX2 and AVX512 are 3.57, 5.76 and 11.23 times compare to the general SHA-256. Finally, by combining both DLP and TLP techniques together, an impressive speedup of more than 60.38 is reported under AVX512 and 6 cores. Although it is lower than the peak parallelism $N * n = 96$, which may due to the memory bandwidth bottleneck for processor. Overall, these results show the good scalability of parallel simulation on the many-core processor, and confirm the advantage of combining DLP and TLP for the overall algorithm's performance.

SIMD Implementation on Different Cache Levels and Main Memory. Intel® Core™ i7-3770 only equip with AVX, here $S_{AVX/General} \approx 3.62$. The results show that hashing from all three cache levels can be performed at roughly the same performance, and there is only some small performance degradation when the data is hashed from the main memory. $S_{AVX/General}$ is a little more than the previous test, which may result to the overhead from cache is more efficient than in the main memory (Fig. 7).

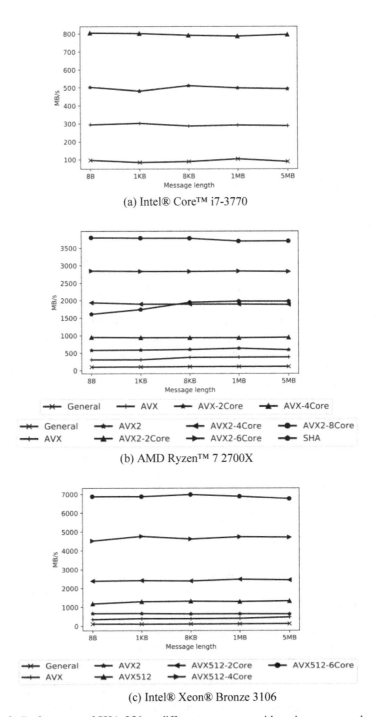

(a) Intel® Core™ i7-3770

(b) AMD Ryzen™ 7 2700X

(c) Intel® Xeon® Bronze 3106

Fig. 6. Performance of SHA-256 on different processors with various message length.

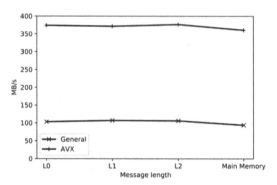

Fig. 7. SHA-256 hashing from different cache levels and memory.

5 Conclusions

This paper proposes two modified SHA-256 approach for different situations and demonstrated the advantage of combining thread-level parallelism (TLP) and data-level parallelism (DLP) architecture together to accelerate SHA-256 in Blockchain applications. The speedups we observe depend on the location of the data and the platform itself, but are significant in all cases. Experiments demonstrate both IMV-MS and the proposed SHA-256 can achieve a significant performance improvement over the present SHA-256 algorithm in Blockchain. This paper is not limited to Bitcoin, any Blockchain applications which use SHA-1 series, SHA-2 series as hash functions can utilize this method, although their computational processes are different in details.

References

1. Federal Information Processing Standards Publication 180-4. https://nvlpubs.nist.gov/nis tpubs/FIPS/NIST.FIPS.180-4.pdf. Accessed 30 Mar 2020
2. Nakamoto, S.: Bitcoin: a peer-to-peer electronic cash system. https://bitcoin.org. Accessed 30 Mar 2020
3. Androulaki, E., Barger, A., Bortnikov, V., Cachin, C., Christidis, K., et al.: Hyperledger fabric: a distributed operating system for permissioned blockchains. In: Proceedings of the Thirteenth EuroSys Conference, pp. 1–15. ACM, New York (2018)
4. Buterin, V.: Ethereum: a next generation smart contract and decentralized application platform. https://github.com/ethereum/wiki/wiki/White-Paper. Accessed 30 Mar 2020
5. Justin, D.: Ethereum 2.0 will use SHA256. https://www.jinse.com/blockchain/336328.html. Accessed 30 Mar 2020
6. Courtois, Nicolas T., Grajek, M., Naik, R.: Optimizing SHA256 in bitcoin mining. In: Kotulski, Z., Księżopolski, B., Mazur, K. (eds.) CSS 2014. CCIS, vol. 448, pp. 131–144. Springer, Heidelberg (2014). https://doi.org/10.1007/978-3-662-44893-9_12
7. Gueron, S., Krasnov, V.: Parallelizing message schedules to accelerate the computations of hash functions. J. Cryptogr. Eng. **2**(4), 241–253 (2012)
8. Guilford, J., Yap, K., Gopal, V.: Fast SHA-256 Implementations on Intel® Architecture Processors Contents. https://www.intel.com/content/dam/www/public/us/en/documents/white-papers/sha-256-implementations-paper.pdf. Accessed 30 Mar 2020

9. Sean, G., Vinodh G., Kirk Y., Wajdi F., Jim G., Gil W.: Intel® SHA Extensions: New Instructions Supporting the Secure Hash Algorithm on Intel® Architecture Processors. https://software.intel.com/sites/default/files/article/402097/intel-sha-extensions-white-paper.pdf. Accessed 30 Mar 2020

10. McEvoy, R.P., Francis, M.C., Colin, C.M., William, P.M.: Optimisation of the SHA-2 family of hash functions on FPGAs. In: Proceedings of the IEEE Computer Society Annual Symposium on Emerging VLSI Technologies and Architectures, pp. 317–322. IEEE, NW Washington (2006)

11. Lien, R., Grembowski, T., Gaj, K.: A 1 Gbit/s partially unrolled architecture of hash functions SHA-1 and SHA-512. In: Okamoto, T. (ed.) CT-RSA 2004. LNCS, vol. 2964, pp. 324–338. Springer, Heidelberg (2004). https://doi.org/10.1007/978-3-540-24660-2_25

12. Taylor, M.B.: The evolution of bitcoin hardware. Computer **50**(9), 58–66 (2017)

13. Jega, A.D.: Bitcoin mining acceleration and performance quantification. In: 2014 IEEE 27th Canadian Conference on Electrical and Computer Engineering, pp. 1–6. IEEE, NW Washington (2014)

14. SIMD. http://simd.sourceforge.net/. Accessed 30 Mar 2020

15. Fang, Z.H., Zheng, B.L., Weng, C.L.: Interleaved multi-vectorizing. Proc. VLDB Endow. **13**(3), 226–238 (2019)

EduChain: A Blockchain-Based Education Data Management System

Yihan Liu[1], Ke Li[1], Zihao Huang[1], Bowen Li[1],
Guiyan Wang[1], and Wei Cai[1,2(✉)]

[1] The Chinese University of Hong Kong, Shenzhen, Shenzhen, China
{yihanliu,keli,zihaohuang,bowenli,guiyanwang}@link.cuhk.edu.cn,
caiwei@cuhk.edu.cn
[2] Shenzhen Institute of Artificial Intelligence and Robotics for Society,
Shenzhen, China

Abstract. The current centralized educational data management system results in problems like malicious tampering, low cost of diploma fabrication, and high cost of certificate verification. The start-of-the-art decentralized blockchain technology can be applied to solve the problems. In this paper, we reveal the shortages of current centralized systems and propose EduChain, a heterogeneous blockchain education data management system, which leverages the advantages of both private blockchains and consortium blockchains. We also propose an effective mechanism to conduct database consistency check and error traceback based on the second consensus via pt-table-checksum tool to solve the database mismatching problem. This system shows good performance in information verification, error traceback and data security.

Keywords: Blockchain · Education · Data management

1 Introduction

Cloud service is the critical technology of smart campus. Nowadays, many universities handle data management in their own data centers. The centralized way of managing data mainly has two negative features: opacity and isolation. The opacity nature means that the access to data is strictly restricted to certain IT staffs without public supervision. The data is likely to be controlled by authorities, which results in malicious tampering [1,13]. The isolation nature means that the data among institutions are scattered and stored without a unified standard. This leads to the high cost of sharing information among departments or institutions. When students have to prove his/her diploma to employers or higher education institutions, problems arise due to the centralized way of data management.

This work was supported by Project 61902333 supported by National Natural Science Foundation of China, by the Shenzhen Institute of Artificial Intelligence and Robotics for Society (AIRS).

© Springer Nature Singapore Pte Ltd. 2021
K. Xu et al. (Eds.): CBCC 2020, CCIS 1305, pp. 66–81, 2021.
https://doi.org/10.1007/978-981-33-6478-3_5

Problems mainly include: 1) Malicious tampering: the centralized system may lead to academic cheating. [1] Certain department like registry owns the absolute authority on students' grades information. Therefore, data can be modified without public supervision of other departments. 2) High cost of verification [12]: the isolation and opacity of data among institutions result in inconvenience and high time/money cost in validating students' transcripts and diplomas. Masses of materials have to be reviewed to ensure the correctness. 3) Great difficulty in accountability and error traceback: the traditional database systems have difficulties operating rollback when errors occur, especially when the records are age-long.

The blockchain technology can be applied to solve the above problems. At present, blockchain technology gradually plays a role in traditional industries like finance, health-care and education. A blockchain is essentially a distributed database of records, or public ledger of all transactions or digital events that have been executed and shared among participating parties [1]. Transactions are recorded into a public distributed ledger. Ledger consists of many blocks. New blocks are added to the chain in chronological order. Once a block is added, it cannot be removed or altered. The cost of modifying a record is enormous because the new block contains the hash value of the previous block [8,9,14]. After both sides achieve a consensus, the transaction can be completed automatically base on the cryptography without a third-party guarantor.

The traditional education blockchain systems usually adopt a single-chain structure, which is limited in information verification. To meet the increasing needs for managing education data in complex situations like proving diploma to foreign institutions, we propose EduChain, a heterogeneous blockchain system by leveraging the advantages of private blockchains and consortium blockchains.

The application of private chains provides a more reliable way to storage all kinds of personal information. The consortium chain serves for recording the commitment, transferring information and verifying the authenticity of information. In addition, to solve the problem that the databases held by different nodes in the private blockchain may mismatch, we propose an effective mechanism to conduct database consistency checking and error tracing based on second consensus via pt-table-checksum tool.

This paper is organized as follows. In part 2, we reviewed the related work of blockchain in education system, including technology features and existing systems. In part 3, we present the overall framework of our system. In part 4, we present the technical design, organization logic, and functions of our system. In part 5, we present the details of how we implement our system. Some codes are displayed for interpretation. In Part 6, we demonstrate our system via real screenshots and compared with others' systems. In the last part, we summary this paper and discuss potential future work.

2   Related Work

2.1   Blockchain Technology

Properties of blockchain secure the transaction environment, which helps a lot in traditional education dilemmas. 1) Blockchain prevents malicious tampering effectively. Blockchain is featured with distributed network, which is decentralized [8,10,11]. Each modification is regarded as a transaction, and is uploaded to the private chain, which can be monitored by all nodes. 2) Combining the transparency of consortium chains and the privacy of private chains, blockchain provides a convenient way to verify students" information with privacy well protected. 3) Each modification is permanently recorded on the blockchain and can be traced back easily, which makes rollback and accountability possible. The key technologies to support the blockchain are distributed consensus and smart contract.

Distributed Consensus. Since the database on blockchain is a distributed ledger, each participant of the P2P network holds a replication of the confirmed shared database. Each of the node has a data pool where the data has not been shared to the network. To make the blockchain valid, the packaged data should conform to a consistent standard on which all nodes agree. This is reached by a consensus protocol [8]. The consensus protocol ensures the validation of block and unifies the structure of data block. The most commonly used consensuses are proof-of-work (PoW), proof-of-stake (PoS) and delegated-proof-of-stake (DPoS) [8].

Smart Contract. Smart contract is the crucial component of getting rid of third-party guarantor. Smart contracts are light but effective programs stored on the blockchain. It automatically executes a transaction in case of presupposed conditions [9]. Therefore, no third party is required to construct the trust system.

2.2   Related Blockchain-Based Education System

The blockchain technology brought possibilities to solve the traditional dilemmas, and many institutes have started their blockchain projects. Learning and reviewing how others build their systems helps us propose and improve our system significantly.

Media Lab Learning Initiative in Massachusetts Institute of Technology (MIT) built a platform for creating, sharing, and verifying the educational certificates [10]. This project focuses on digitizing and verifying the academic certificates. Some details like credit transferring are not considered. It does not perform well in globalization because only some domestic universities used this system.

EduCTX [11] is a global platform used for issuing educational certificates and credit transferring. It included European Credit Transfer and Accumulation System (ECTS). However, this system does not have the ability to verify the detailed academic records. Thus they cannot prevent malicious tampering and diploma fabrication.

A solution of Haojian Shen and Yohuan Xiao [12] solved the online quiz problems that the score process is non-transparent, injustice and the final results are easy to be modified. This system, contrary to the previous systems, focuses on small quizzes and exams so that it cannot verify the educational certificates.

3   System Overview

As one of the most popular topics in the computer areas, blockchain has already been applied to many industries. The properties of high redundancy, unchangeable, traceable, transparency, as well as the security provided by private blockchain of blockchain, are essential to the education data area.

3.1   Objective

Compared with a traditional centralized database, EduChain provides another way to store education information for universities. EduChain stores each modification of education information, like student information, staff information, and so on, in the private blockchain supported by each university. Each node of private blockchain was maintained by a single department of the university. And, each node maintains a relational database to store the final state of the education information. In case of data inconsistency of the final-state-database among different nodes, either caused by software or hardware, EduChain uses pt-table-checksum, an online replication consistency check tool, to conduct the second consensus and fix the inconsistency by tracking the source.

In addition to the data storage, EduChain also provides a method for universities and recruiters to share information fast and safely. The commitments of students" personal information will be uploaded into the consortium blockchain regularly. A commitment scheme is a cryptography primitive that allows committing to a chosen value (or chosen statement) while keeping it hidden to others, with the ability to reveal the committed value later [2]. Here in our design logic, the commitment is a string that was calculated by the SHA256 algorithm.

3.2   Framework

As shown in Fig. 1, our system consists of 3 major layers: blockchain platform layer, front-end layer and user interface layer.

Blockchain Platform. The Blockchain platform layer mainly consisted of several virtual nodes based on cloud technology. By utilizing the private blockchain and consortium blockchain technology, all the nodes are connected to a network. This layer provides APIs for the front-end layer to read and write data, APIs for data comparison and mistake tracking, and APIs for the administrators to manually fix the mistakes.

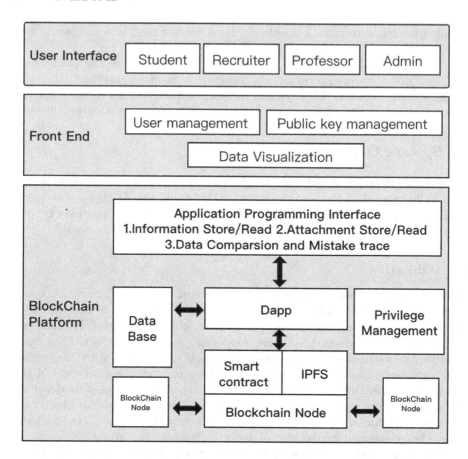

Fig. 1. Framework of EduChain

The Blockchain platform layer has the following components: one consortium blockchain and several private blockchains. Different blockchain stores different information. The consortium blockchain is maintained by the Ministry of Education together with many universities. Each private blockchain is maintained by one university only. All the education information will be stored into the node of the private blockchain. The normal relational information will be stored into a relational database, while for large attachments like photos will be stored in IPFS. IPFS is the abbreviation of The Inter Planetary File System, which is a peer-to-peer distributed file system that seeks to connect all computing devices with the same system of files [3]. IPFS provides a safe and efficient way to store huge attachments.

In the consortium blockchain, each university and the Ministry of Education should make a consensus on the records in the blockchain. Two kinds of information will be uploaded to the consortium blockchain. One is the commitment of important information like transcript and diploma. The consortium blockchain can provide a website maintained by the Ministry of Education for people who need to certificate academic information. This method fulfills the requirements of certificating the student information and meanwhile protects the privacy. Another classification of information is the request and commitment of the shared information between universities. For example, A student takes summer session in another school. When he wants to transfer his credits, he can use the consortium blockchain. The summer session school will send a request to the student"s school through the consortium blockchain using a smart contract. Then a temporary communication channel will be built, and the transcript will be sent through the channel. This method keeps the authenticity of the transcript and protects the private information of the students. The private blockchain does the second consensus regularly to make sure each database in the different nodes is in consensus. Each node in private blockchain also provides permission management. Different users will have different permissions.

Front-End Layer. The Front-end layer is a gateway for users to get access to the private blockchain. This layer provides the functions of user management, public key management, and data visualization. The front-end layer distributes the requests from users of different departments to their respective nodes. After receiving the response from different nodes, the layer will do the data visualization and deliver the results to the corresponding user interface.

User Interface Layer. User Interface layer is mainly handled with user interaction and page logic. This layer interacts with the front-end layer. The staff user can use this layer to upload and modify the grade of the course. The student user can check the course information and download the transcripts. All the queries, modification, and data upload requests will be sent from the front-end layer to corresponding nodes. When doing modifying and uploading, the requests need to be signed by the user.

4 System Design and Functions

4.1 System Design

Our work is mainly focused on designing an Education information management system based on Heterogeneous blockchainBy utilizing the advantage of a different kind of blockchain, we designed an education information management system which increased the safety of storage, sharing, modification of education information. And, this system also provides high efficiency and reliability. It provides a more reliable and straightforward method to display the student information to the recruiters and the graduate schools. The system offers a convenient way for the user to verify information while keeping the information itself unreachable. Meanwhile, our system utilizes the online replication consistency check tool pt-table-checksum combined with the second consensus to make sure the consensus of the nodes and provide a way for mistake tracing.

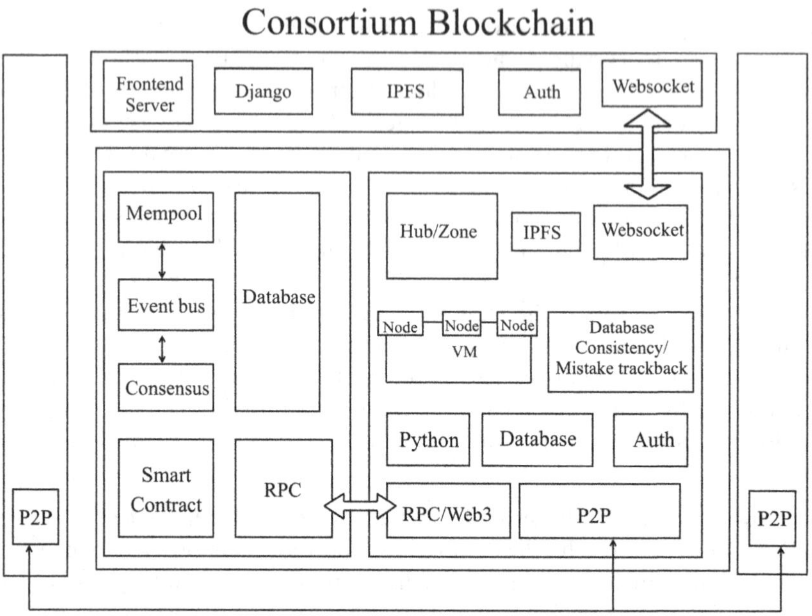

Consortium Blockchain

Fig. 2. Syetem design of consortium chain

In our system, we use the Heterogeneous blockchain technology to combine the private blockchain and consortium blockchain. The consortium blockchain used is hyperledger, while the private blockchain used is Ethereum. The whole system is shown in the Fig. 2.

The whole system can be divided into three major parts: the front-end server, private blockchain, and consortium blockchain. The private blockchain can then divided into smaller parts, Dapp, which means distributed application, and blockchain program. Following are the introduction of the components in our system.

1) Django. Django is a widely used website construction framework, which is used to build a web server. 2) IPFS. IPFS is the abbreviation of The InterPlanetary File System, which is a peer-to-peer distributed file system that seeks to connect all computing devices with the same system of files. 3) Auth. Auth is an identity certification and user management module. In the web server, it refers to the module that identity certification of users. In the node of a private blockchain, it refers to the module that provides authority management function. 4) WebSocket. WebSocket is a network protocol that defines how servers and clients communicate over the Web [4]. 5) VM. VM is the abbreviation of the virtual machine. We use cloud technology to build the nodes, and all those nodes are virtual nodes rather than real nodes. 6) Database consistency. Database consistency is a module to find out whether the databases are consistent or not. 7) Mistake traceback. Mistake traceback is a module to figure out the source of the inconsistency of the database on different nodes. 8) Hub. The hub is a component that connects

different blockchain system. 9) Database. Database is used to store the final state of all the information. The database we used here is MySQL. 10) PRC. Remote procedure calls (RPC) are a useful paradigm for providing communication across a network between programs written in a high level language [5]. 11) web3. web3 is serious about the API supplied by Ethereum to make the Dapp interact with the Ethereum network. 12) Mempool. Mempool is the module to store the committed transaction temporarily. 13) Event bus. Event bus is used to transact the information between mempool module and the consensus module. 14) Consensus. Consensus is a module for making consensus in the blockchain system. In our design, the private chain uses Pow to make consensus, while consortium blockchain uses Kafka to make consensus. 15) Kafka. Kafka is a distributed messaging system that we developed for collecting and delivering high volumes of log data with low latency [6]. 16) POW. POW is the abbreviation of proof-of-work, which is a consensus algorithm. 17) Smart contract. A smart contract is a programmed functionality which executes some part of the legal contract [7].

4.2   Functions

The functions provided by the whole system can be categorized into six characters: private chain data querying, private chain data modification, attachment uploading, consortium blockchain synchronizing, the verification of important student information, database consistency checking and mistake tracing. The logic of the first three functions is shown in Fig. 3.

I. Private Chain Data Query. The user first sends the request to the front-server. The front-end server sends the user request to the corresponding nodes. Later on, the node of the private blockchain will send back the results to the front-end server. Then, the front-end server will conduct the visualization processes and send the results back to the user.

II. Private Chain Data Modification. The user first sends the request to the front-server. The front-end server sends the user request to the corresponding node based on the department of the user by using the user management module. The private node server then calls the smart-contract to conduct the modification. Every node on the private blockchain uses a filter to monitor the events that happen on the private blockchain. When the modification event is watched, the node on the private blockchain will then modify the final state database and send the results back to the front-end server, and then back to the user.

III. Attachments Uploading. The front-end server first receives the attachment and saves it through the IPFS. Later on, the front-end server will send the reference of the attachment to the corresponding nodes. The private node server then calls the smart-contract to conduct the uploading. When the uploading event is watched, the node on the private blockchain will then modify the final state database and send the result back to the front-end server, and then back to the user.

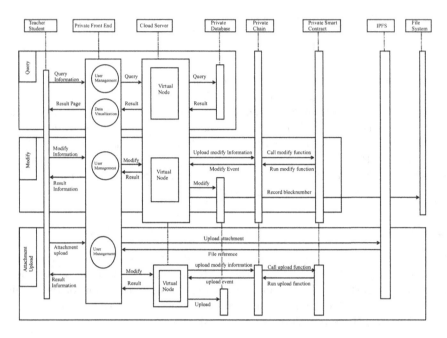

Fig. 3. Logic of function I, II, III

IV. Consortium Blockchain Synchronizing. The university maintains a special node. This node will not be assigned to tasks like data querying, modification, or attachment uploading. This node will be regarded as a so-called huba node that runs both the private blockchain and consortium blockchain. The node works as a connection between a private blockchain and consortium blockchain. It will upload the related data from the private blockchain to the consortium blockchain. The hub will first take the data from the final state database, then hash the data to a string. The hub will then call the smart-contract on the consortium blockchain to upload the hash string to the consortium blockchain.

V. Verification of Important Student Information. There is a special node maintained by the Ministry of Education, which is the only node in the consortium blockchain that never connects to a private blockchain. A front-end server is constructed on this node. When the recruiter needs to verify some information, they only need to upload the information to the front-end server. The node will hash the information to a string, and compare the result with the hash string in the database, then send the result back to the user.

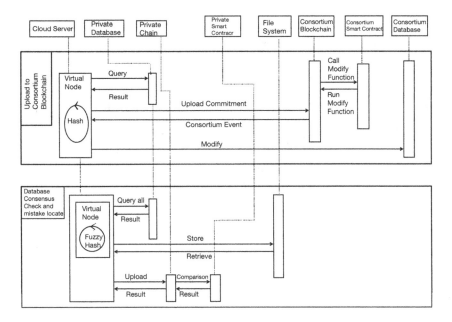

Fig. 4. Logic of function IV

VI. Database Consistency Checking and Mistake Tracing. Due to the discrete nature of the blockchain system, the same database content will be scattered on different nodes. In our design, in order to obtain efficient data acquisition and modification, we store the final state of the data of each node in the relational database MySQL data. However, a new problem arises. The data stored in the MySQL database deviates from the data structure of the blockchain, and the consensus mechanism of the blockchain will no longer act on such independent relational data.

In order to ensure the consistency of this data, we combined the md5 verification algorithm, pt-table-checksum MySQL master-slave database consistency detection tool, and smart contracts to implement a consistency detection and error tracing of the database on different nodes. This method uses the md5 verification algorithm to calculate the verification value of each database and conducts a second consensus by voting in the form of a blockchain to select the consensus database state. If there is data inconsistency in a database, the pt-table-checksum tool will trace the error. Thanks to the characteristics of the private chain, the cost of the second consensus will become bearable.

5   System Implementation

5.1   Selection of Platform

In order to meet the functional requirements, we have selected a series of packages to develop prototypes. For the database, we chose MySQL for development.

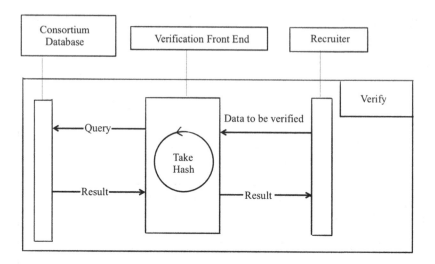

Fig. 5. Logic of function V

MySQL is a lightweight, free, and open-source database that is compatible with all mainstream platforms and is suitable for prototype development. For the private blockchain part, we developed it on the Ethereum platform. Ethereum is a decentralized open-source blockchain featuring smart contract functionality platform.

As for the consortium chain, we used Hyperledger fabric. Hyperledger has a relatively complete verification mechanism, which provides a safe and reliable guarantee for the identity verification of the nodes added to the alliance chain. Based on this choice, we used python for smart contract development in the consortium chain, and solidity for smart contract development in the private chain.

To support the rapid development of the front end, we chose the Django framework and developed the central part of the prototype based on python. For the interaction with the blockchain, we use web3.py, a python package that provides interaction with Ethereum. For the cloud platform, we chose AWS"s VPC service and created five EC2 virtual services to build the network. AWS is a cloud platform developed by Amazon, which provides high-quality services and is very suitable for prototype development.

5.2   Prototype Deployment

We deployed our prototype on the AWS VPC with 5 EC2 instances. The smart contracts are tested using the Remix online tool without running on the real Ethereum network. We designed two kinds of smart contracts. The first one provides the interfaces for query and modifies the related information. It also record each operation of the data into the blockchain. The second smart contract provides the interfaces for a administrator to check the consistency of all the databases and to locate mistakes. We also use the CodeAnyWhere online editor to deploy our front end. To fulfill the requirements of our system, we deployed the private blockchain using the configuration set up by ourselves.

As shown in the code block below, our system follow the Byzantium hard fork starting from the first block. To fulfill the requirement of QoS and reduce the latency, we set the difficulty extremely low, which means that we can have a new block in a short time.

```
 1  {
 2    "config":{
 3    "byzantiumBlock":0,
 4    "chainID":5421,
 5    "homesteadBlock":0,
 6    "eip150Block":0,
 7    "eip155Block":0,
 8    "eip158Block":0
 9    },
10    "coinbase":"0x0000000000000000000000000000000000000000",
11    "difficulty":"0x400",
12    "extraData":"0x5421",
13    "gasLimit":"0xffffffffffff",
14    "nonce":"0xdeadbeefdeadbeef",
15    "mixhash":"0x0000000000000000000000000000000000000000
16            00000000000000000000",
17    "parentHash":"0x000000000000000000000000000000000000000
18            0000000000000000000000000",
19    "timestamp":"0x00",
20    "alloc":{}
21    }
22  }
```

Besides, the gas limitation for each block is set to be a high value. In other words, we can contain more transactions in one single block. Then, we started the Ethereum network using the command shown in the code below (The code is in one single line).

```
1  geth —identity "EDU" —rpc —rpcport "8545"
2  —datadir data —allow−insecure−unlock —port
3  "30303" —rpcapi "miner,debug,personal,db,eth,
4  net,web3" —networkid 5421 —maxpeers 7 console
```

6   Performance

6.1   Demonstration

After the user logs in the EduChain account, he/she is able to visit MyProfile through the left tool module. The personal information for this account is

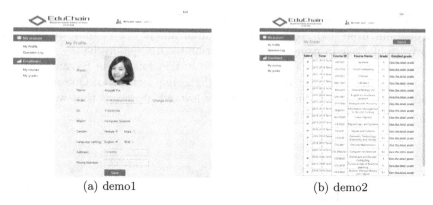

(a) demo1   (b) demo2

displayed on this web page, as shown in Fig. 6. The user could change his personal information such as telephone, email, and address, which is stored in the corresponding node"s Inter Planetary File System and database.

For students, their course grades are demonstrated in Mygrade web page, which is illustrated in Fig. 7. Students can click the attached URL to view the detailed assessment. If a student wants to export an official transcript from this web page, he first needs to tick the check-box to select the courses in the generated transcript. Then, the student clicks the Export button to generate a request to the central server. Moreover, the user"s password will be needed in this process to authenticate his identity. A download URL of this transcript will be notified after successful identification.

Fig. 6. demo3

As for teaching staff, the Educhain system provides an approach to modify the students final grades. Once the staff has submitted the grades, it will send a transaction request to the server. After identification, the node server will receive and verify the digital signature. The private chain of this node will record this modification, and Dapp will synchronize the modified database with the other databases on this private chain.

For each account, there is an operation log stored in the node file system. We also design an operation log web page, as Fig. 6 shown, which presents the users" operation detail, such as the start time and block numbers. Combined with the database consistency checking and error tracing mechanism, the operation log could quickly handle the database mismatch problem between nodes on the private chain.

6.2 Comparison with Other Similar Systems

	MIT Digital Certificates	Shen's System	EduCTX	EduChain
Digitized Certificate	√		√	√
Certificate Verification	√		√	√
Course Grade		√	√	√
Detailed Grade Trace		√		√
Support for Globalization			√	√

Fig. 7. Comparison with MIT's, Shen's and EduCTX Systems

As mentioned in the related work section, MIT Digital project focuses on digitizing certificates. It did not investigate into global usage. EduCTX is a global-used platform. It can not only digitize and verify certificates, but also have the record of course history. However, it does not support detailed course grade trace, which means it cannot prevent record-fabrication before final grade came out. Shen"s online quiz system can help to avoid quiz-cheating, but this light system does not support high level functions like certificate verification. EduChain can digitize certificates and verify them. At the same time, it offers course history information and detailed course grades. Moreover, the consortium blockchain provides the foundation of globalization.

7 Conclusions and Future Work

This paper presents the design and implementation of the heterogeneous blockchain system, which can be used to verify information, secure the data and trace the error. The significance of this system mainly lies in: 1) It combines the advantages of private blockchains and consortium blockchains, which provides a more reliable and efficient method to storage and verify all kinds of information. 2) Based on second consensus, we propose a fast and effective mechanism to conduct database consistency checking and error tracing via pttable-checksum, which is quite helpful when the databases mismatch with each other in the private blockchain. However, data redundancy arises from the design that each node holds its own databases. Future work can focus on how to reduce data redundancy with data security ensured.

References

1. Wang, G.Y., Zhangand, H.B., Xiao, B.W., Chung, Y.C.: EduBloud: a blockchain-based education cloud. In: 2019 Computing, Communications and IoT Applications (ComComAp), Shenzhen, China, pp. 352–357. https://doi.org/10.1109/ComComAp46287.2019.9018818
2. Sharples, M., Domingue, J.: The Blockchain and Kudos: a distributed system for educational record, reputation and reward. In: Verbert, K., Sharples, M., Klobučar, T. (eds.) EC-TEL 2016. LNCS, vol. 9891, pp. 490–496. Springer, Cham (2016). https://doi.org/10.1007/978-3-319-45153-4_48
3. Benet, J.: IPFS - Content Addressed, Versioned, P2P File System (DRAFT 3). eprint arXiv (2014)
4. Wang, V., Salim, F., Moskovits, P.: The WebSocket protocol. In: The Definitive Guide to HTML5 WebSocket. Apress, Berkeley (2013). https://doi.org/10.1007/978-1-4302-4741-8_3
5. Birrell, A.D., Nelson, B.J.: Implementing remote procedure calls. In: Proceedings of the 9th ACM Symposium on Operating Systems Principles-SOSP 1983, New York (1983). https://doi.org/10.1145/800217.806609
6. Jay, K., Narkhede, N., Rao, J.: Kafka: a distributed messaging system for log processing. In: Proceedings of the ACM SIGMOD Workshop on Networking Meets Databases, New York (2012)
7. Kõlvart, M., Poola, M., Rull, A.: Smart contracts. In: Kerikmäe, T., Rull, A. (eds.) The Future of Law and eTechnologies, pp. 133–147. Springer, Cham (2016). https://doi.org/10.1007/978-3-319-26896-5_7
8. Zheng, Z., Xie, S., Dai, H., Chen, X., Wang, H.: An overview of blockchain technology: architecture, consensus, and future trends. In: IEEE International Congress on Big Data (BigData Congress), pp. 557–564 (2017)
9. Grech, A., Camilleri, A.F.: Blockchain in Education. Publications Office of the European Union, Luxembourg (2017)
10. Media Lab Learning Initiative. Digital Certificates Project. http://certificates.media.mit.edu/
11. Turkanović, M., Hölbl, M., Košič, K., Heričko, M., Kamišalić, A.: EduCTX: a blockchain-based higher education credit platform. IEEE Access 1, 5112–5127 (2018). https://doi.org/10.1109/ACCESS.2018.2789929

12. Shen, H., Xiao, Y.: Research on online quiz scheme based on double-layer consortium blockchain. In: 2018, 9th International Conference on Information Technology in Medicine and Education (ITME), Hangzhou, pp. 956–960 (2018). https://doi.org/10.1109/ITME.2018.00213
13. Taghavi, M., Bentahar, J., Otrok, H., Bakhtiyari, K.: A blockchain-based model for cloud service quality monitoring. IEEE Trans. Serv. Comput. **13**(2), 276–288 (2020). https://doi.org/10.1109/TSC.2019.2948010
14. Bernstein, D., Demchenko, Y.: The IEEE intercloud testbed - creating the global cloud of clouds. In: Proceedings of the 2013 IEEE International Conference on Cloud Computing Technology and Science, vol. 2 (2013). https://doi.org/10.1109/CloudCom.2013.102

A Case Study for Blockchain in OTC: "BATN": A Prototype for Bid and Ask Trading Network

Qing Zhang[1], Jian Gao[1], Qiqiang Qin[1], and Keting Yin[2(✉)]

[1] Shanghai Financial Futures Information Technology Co., Ltd., Shanghai, China
644413421@qq.com, {gaojian,qinqq}@cffex.com.cn
[2] College of Software Technology, Zhejiang University, Hangzhou, China
yinkt@zju.edu.cn

Abstract. With product iteration and emerging market demand, traditional organizations have to look for ways to exchange information and trade options/swaps under trust-less network. In this paper, we propose – "BATN": a prototype for bid and ask trading network based on Blockchain. We propose a system in which a decentralized network of trading agencies, supervisor institutions and witness nodes can enable public bid/ask, automated risk evaluation, and transparent supervision through a trail of historic trading behavior and smart contracts. Our system decentralizes critical information about alliance governance, authentication and credit evaluation through a verifiable audit trail. We present BATN using Hyperchain through which a consortium of geographically dispersed organizations can operate business, sign e-contracts and report transactions anywhere and anytime. Our prototype makes sure the transaction per second on a decentralized network can meet trading volume in reality. This paper intends to improve business effectiveness for much larger fields through the working prototype and discusses the potential of blockchain for finance IT.

Keywords: Bid and ask · Alliance governance · Authentication · Credit · Smart contract

1 Introduction

The OTC (Over-The-Counter) market is the cornerstone to financial market. The OTC market not only offers ways for raising funds for institutions, but also provides vehicles for investors.

In September 2009, the G20 leaders reached an agreement in Pittsburgh: All standardized OTC derivatives should be traded through exchanges or electronic trading systems. What's more, all standardized OTC derivatives should be clearing though central counterparty before the end of 2012. According to Financial Stability Board (FSB), as of September 2019, 13 countries and regions have meet the requirement that standardized derivatives be traded on electronic trading systems [1]. The overseas OTC trading system has three characteristics. Firstly, multi-party participation. Their system breaks one-to-one negotiation pattern to promote price bid and ask efficiency. Secondly, sufficient competition. Full order books, frequent bid and ask together make high market liquidity. Thirdly, market transparency. Trading elements is access to all candidates.

China's OTC market is developing fast since 2014. As of OTC option, the size is 11.5 trillion RMB in 2014 and 1255.6 trillion RMB in 2019. Figure 1 shows the development of China's OTC market from 2014 to 2019. However, in China the cumulative size of OTC market is only half of the exchange market. According to Bank for International Settlements (BIS), by the end of 2019 the size of global OTC market size is approximately 5.8 times larger than that of the exchange market [2].

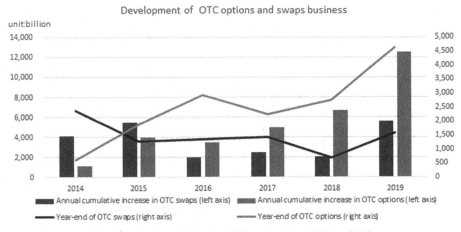

Fig. 1. The size of China's OTC market from 2014 to 2019

China's OTC market is complex in participants. Various agencies plays different rules in registration, custody, clearing and settlement. They are heavy in exchange information. For various reasons, China's OTC market is not transparent enough. Customers are not easy to get the best price in the market. Besides, breaches occur from time to time. Participants lack effective tools to handle counterparties' default risk.

An option to solve problems above is to establish a unified exchange, where services can be accessed in one platform. However, balancing the interests of all parties is impossible. Besides, they are not ready to abandon existing trading infrastructures.

An alternative implementation would be to build platforms that are decentralized where all participants can fair share business information and conduct trusted transactions in the platform ecosystem. The transparency offered by decentralization, the value offered through broadcast bid/ask and the trust guaranteed by multi-party computation together form the cornerstone of the platform.

This paper focuses on a system framework though which a decentralized network of all parties can operate in a decentralized bid and ask trading network called BATN. We have highlighted the following areas where blockchain technology make sense compared to current practice in the OTC market. First, BATN establishes alliance governance for long-term development. The sponsors are elected to the Governance Committee. The Governance Committee is the highest authority among all parties. Second, the smart contract is widely adopted in BATP. The smart contract demonstrates how instructions can be sent to participants. Once conditions are met within the code rule, the smart contract automatically drives trading business. Lastly, all information are transparent in BATP. Supervisors can trust the trading report while participants can trust each other based on their historical trading behavior.

2   Related Works

In recent years, scholars have studied the application of financial markets using blockchain.

In August 2015, the smart contract system named Symbiont announced the first issuance of smart bonds. This marked the substantial progress in the application of smart contracts in the bond market [3].

In October 2017, a Russian telecommunications operator named Megafon had already taken issued 500 million rubles of blockchain-based bonds, bypassing traditional bond issuers such as investment banks [4].

In August 2018, the Commonwealth Bank of Australia and the World Bank issued the first blockchain bank bonds based on the Ethereum public blockchain. The first blockchain bank bonds are groundbreaking. It proves that blockchain technology can satisfy different participants from issuers to dealers and implement full-cycle management [5].

In April 2019, Societe Generale announced that it had issued approximately $112 million bonds in the form of tokens on the Ethereum public blockchain [6].

In September 2019, the Spanish bank Santander released its first bond fully operated by blockchain technology on the Ethereum public blockchain system, valued at $200 million. Thai Bank also said that the Thai bond market is preparing to implement regional blockchain technology and launch its own crypto currency [7].

In November 2019, HSBC announced that tokens together with smart contracts on the private blockchain is used to share data among organizations and track the life cycle of bonds. DLT helps to solve the problem of inefficient during bond issuance and redemption [8].

In late 2019, the Bank of Korea launched a proof-of-concept project to move the bond transaction records currently maintained by the Korea Securities Depository to a blockchain-backed record repository accessed by multiple nodes [9].

Domestic banks and experts are also concerned about using blockchain on bonds. In December 2019, the Bank of China announced they had completed the issuance and pricing of the first 20 billion RMB financial bonds for small and micro enterprises [10].

We have also completed the OTC Option Management and Trading System on consortium blockchain, which proves the feasibility of financial transactions [11].

Based on our works, we put forward BATN to build a standardized derivatives trading system.

3   System Design and Implementation

3.1   Business Process

The lifecycle of OTC derivatives is shown in Fig. 2.

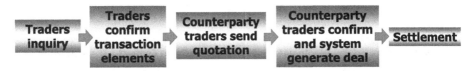

Fig. 2. The basic process of OTC derivatives trading

Traders use the Internet or telephone to find potential trading parties through brokers. The inquiry process called bid/ask. Once potential parties are determined, both sides will bargain to reach an agreement on trading elements, such as price, quantity, time limit, and settlement method etc. After all elements are agreed, the counterparty trader sends a quotation to the trader. The quotation sets transaction direction, variety, price, quantity, deadline, settlement method, and settlement speed on the e-contract. If the trader or the counterparty trader confirms, then he will click to deal. The system will generate deal and inform supervisors once both sides confirmed the same e-contract. The back office transfers money according to the deal.

3.2   System Architecture

BATN is divided into four layers, as shown in Fig. 3.

1) *First Layer: Blockchain Layer.*

The Blockchain Layer is the foundation. We choose Hyperchain developed and owned by Hangzhou Qulian Technology [12]. The first layer contains HyperVM, consensus algorithm, ledger and P2P network. HyperVM allows smart contracts run everywhere. The consensus algorithm is called Byzantine Fault Tolerance and capable of allowing 1/3 nodes' failure on the Blockchain. Users can choose different databases for the ledger.

2) *Second Layer: Core Service Layer.*

The Core Service Layer carries main functions of BATN. We implement governance module, CA module, storage module, e-contract module and supervisor module here. The governance module provides governance rules on BATN. The CA module provides authentication for both individual users and institutional users. The storage module is used to store business data. The e-contract module is to provide electronic signature and contract signing. The supervisor module allows supervisors to handle all transactions on BATN and conduct immediate measures.

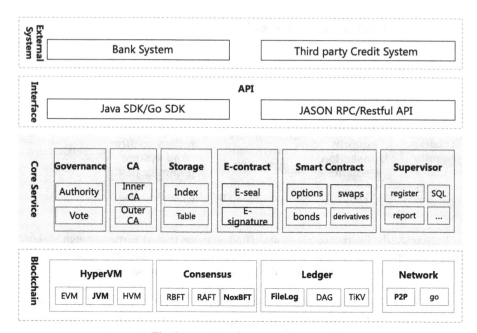

Fig. 3. System architecture of BATN

3) *Third Layer: Interface Layer.*

The Interface Layer is used to linked with external systems such as banks and credit rating agencies.

4) *Fourth Layer: External system Layer.*

The External System Layer is for external systems. BATN needs to connect with banks and credit rating agencies.

3.3 Consensus Algorithm

As mentioned in Sect. 3.2, the consensus algorithm is RBFT. RBFT reduces the traffic of the broadcast strategically by forwarding to Primary instead of broadcasting to the full-network. The nodes are divided into Primary node and Replica nodes. The Primary node is in charge of validating transactions while the Replica nodes validate and sort the transactions. There is only one Primary node any time on BATN. Once a consensus procedure achieved, the data and status of Primary node and Replica nodes stay the same. If the Primary node is out of service, a new Primary node will be elected.

Suppose there are 3f+1 nodes in blockchain network. RBFT can tolerate f nodes' failure at most. the Primary node manages transactions in sequence. Replica nodes are backup.

The consensus process is shown in Fig. 4. In Transaction stage, a client sends the transaction via connected node. In Batch stage, Replica 3 receives the transaction and broadcasts the transaction to Primary 1 instead of all nodes. Primary 1 receives the transaction and verifies it. Once verified Primary 1 batch processes all transactions and package them in sequence. In PrePrepare Stage, Primary 1 broadcasts the packaged transactions to all nodes. In Prepare Stage, all Replicas receive the packaged transactions and send Prepare message to other nodes, if Replica agrees with the batching and ordering result of Primary 1. In Commit stage, if Replica receives 2f Prepare messages and verifies the legality from Primary 1 the Replica will send Commit messages to other nodes. In Write Back stage, if Replica receives 2f+1 Commit messages, it means all nodes reach a consensus. Replicas will call transaction executor and compare it with the result from Primary. Once verified, the results are written into the ledger.

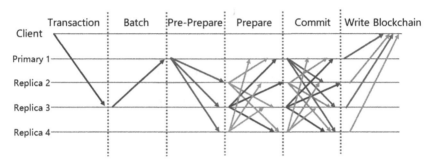

Fig. 4. The consensus of RBFT Algorithm

The benefits of adopting RBFT is obvious. First, after receiving a new transaction, Replica nodes forward the message to the Primary node instead of the entire network and that reduces the bandwidth consumption. Second, the illegal transactions will be removed if the Primary finishes validation. It makes sure that illegal transactions do not consume the blockchain network computing power. Therefore, by applying RBFT, Hyperchain can effectively alleviate the burden of the whole network.

According to experiments, RBFT help Consortium Blockchain achieve a performance of 10000 transactions per second and with an average transaction delay of 300 ms.

At present, Hyperchain uses NoxBFT which reduces the network complexity from $O(n^2)$ to $O(n)$. NoxBFT now supports large-scale expansion of thousands of nodes. In the standard production environment (8-core 16G, standard server of HDD mechanical hard disk) Hyperchain can support 32000TPS (transaction per second) with single chain reaching more than 50000TPS under hardware acceleration.

4   The Specific Program

4.1   Governance

Governance is foundation for ensure stable and smooth operation. We introduce a double layer governance structure in Fig. 5. As time goes on, BATN needs updating. New nodes wait to join while old nodes leave. Even the smart contract may no longer meets new regulatory rules. All parties together from BATN member congress. Based on voluntariness, equality, and cooperation, the member congress elect BATN governance committee. Governance committee is composed of two units. The daily executive agency is responsible for daily operation and maintenance, and the emergency execution agency is responsible for emergency changes.

Fig. 5. The governance structure of BATN

4.2 Authentication

According to Financial Distributed Ledger Technical Security Specification issued by People's Bank of China, a blockchain system should implement effective user identity management, including identity registration, identity verification, account management, credential life cycle management, identity authentication, identity update, and revocation [13].

For individual users there are three ways to finish real name authentication, as shown in Fig. 6. The most convenient is to get an EID from the Ministry of Public Security. Besides, individual users can choose either a bank or a communication operator for authentication.

For institutional users, there are two ways to finish authentication as shown in Fig. 7. They can either use electronic business license, bank account and legal person identity or provide certifications from national authoritative security certification agencies.

4.3 E-contracts

How to prevent from defaults and provide legal evidence when defaults occur? We have been thinking about solving the problems through e-contracts. This paper disassemble the life process of e-contracts signing as shown in Fig. 8. The process can be divided into verification, willingness certification, e-contracts generation and judicial evidence.

We have discussed the individual and institutional authentication in Sect. 4.2. To confirm the will of signers, this paper combine SMS verification code with private key confirmation. Both parties need to put electronic signatures in sequence. To improve security and validity of data records, the judiciary will be invited on BATN.

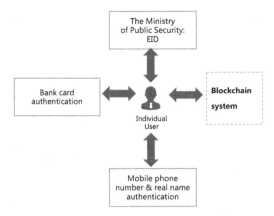

Fig. 6. Authentication of an individual user

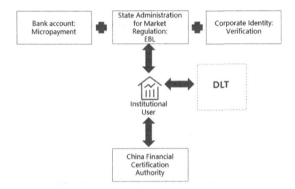

Fig. 7. Authentication of an institutional user

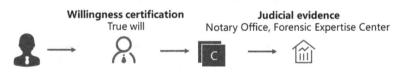

Fig. 8. The process of an e-contract signing

4.4 Bid and Ask Transaction

The transaction procedure is shown in Fig. 9. Suppose A is intend to sell an OTC option at 100.00 RMB. The inquiry is valid for the next half an hour. The information is broadcasted on BATN. Suppose B is looking for this option. B clicks and confirms all conditions. The transaction is sent to the Primary node. The process of consensus is given in Sect. 3.3. Suppose A and B reach an agreement. The transaction is completed automatically by smart contract. Finally, both the transaction and the e-contract are reported to the supervisor.

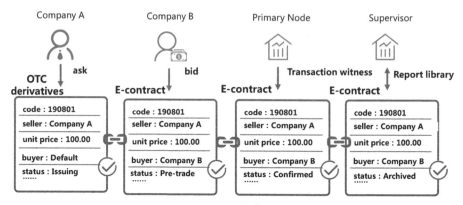

Fig. 9. OTC derivatives trading procedure

4.5 Smart Contract

Smart contract can reduce artificial operations thus helping accelerating the clearing and settlement processes. A smart contract is shown in Fig. 10.

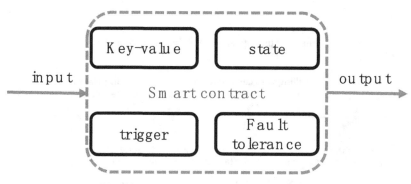

Fig. 10. Inputs and outputs of smart contract

1) Smart contract is adopted to reduce artificial operations, such as verification by intermediaries in traditional trading platform.
2) Smart contract atomically generates e-contracts. Smart contract can handle trading elements on e-contracts from simple parameters like date, price and volume, to arithmetic or logical expression.
3) Smart contract uses standardized codes which improve the efficiency of regulatory.

4) Smart contract builds a completely new credit system. Credit asymmetry is the source of risk. Traditional credit system based on third-party credit rating agencies is beneficial for large enterprises. Smart contract devotes to establish a credit system based on historical transactions and peer evaluation, which better reflects the reality.
5) Last but not the least, smart contract is helpful to penetrating supervision. All information are sent to the supervisor.

In conclusion, smart contract increases reliability, controllability, and transaction efficiency for BATN.

4.6 Hybrid Storage

According to Financial Distributed Ledger Technical Security Specifications mentioned above in Sect. 4.2, BATN chooses mixed databases. On BATN, data is stored differently according its type, as shown in Fig. 11. The public data includes hash of blocks, transactions and e-contracts. These data is either encrypted or public on blockchain. The rest data including account data, transaction data, configuration data, and credit data is stored locally on database in encryption form. For the convenience of search and inquiry, this paper combines public data and private data with index. This hybrid storage is useful to locate business data with its corresponding public data. Both The performance and the privacy of data are guaranteed.

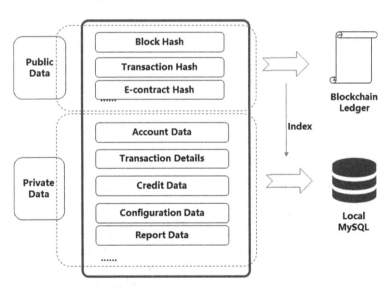

Fig. 11. Hybrid storage architecture

5 Prototype Implementation and Evaluation

In this section, our purpose is to provide a view of BATN and test its performance. Figures 12 and 13 are the view from administrator and business operator. In Fig. 12, we provide administrator with account management, sub-account management, agreement template, signed customer, dealers, data report, volatility, governance, ledger, and watch lists.

Fig. 12. System administrator on BATN

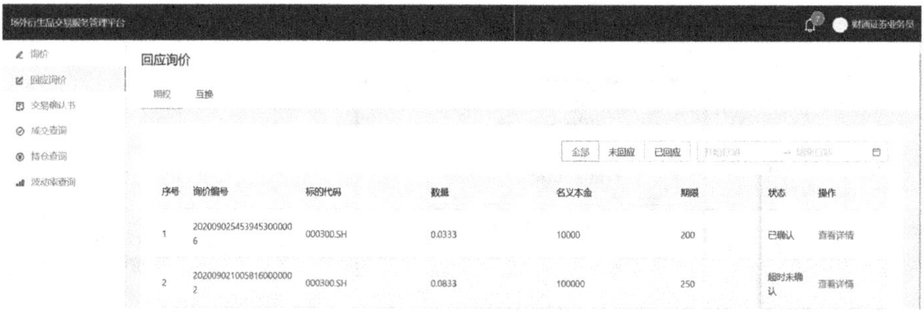

Fig. 13. Business operator on BATN

In Fig. 13, we provide business operator with ask, bid, confirmation, deal, position and volatility.

The experiment uses 5 servers with 4 blockchain nodes and 1 application server. All servers are the same in configuration with 8 core, 16G memory and 500G hard drive. We use Hyperchain 1.6.15 and MySQL 14.14. The experiments conducted are in two perspectives: transaction per second and the latency. The result is shown in Fig. 14. FutureOTC completes 1000 to 1400 transaction per second and its corresponding latency is around 500 to 800 ms. Considering the frequency of the existing OTC market, BATN can meet the daily needs in a foreseen future.

6   Conclusion and Future Work

In this paper, we present a bid and ask trading network – "BATN" based on blockchain. BATN establishes alliance governance to union different nodes and institutions. BATN

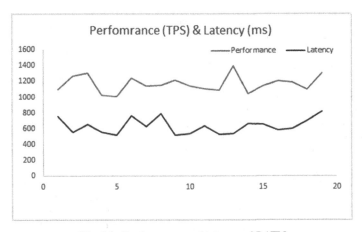

Fig. 14. Performance and latency of BATN

simplifies authentication traditionally completed by intermediaries and agents, thus accelerating the process of OTC trading, improving clearing and settlement efficiency. BATN takes advantage of existing authentication facility to solve the problem of authentication. This paper puts up a standard process for signing e-contracts. In addition, we use smart contracts to accelerate trading process and strengthen supervision. By adopting hybrid storage method, we successfully isolate public data with private data.

Although the application of decentralized system in the OTC market help institutions save the cost of finding intermediaries, issuing OTC products have to go through strict credit rating and follow rigorous review processes. With blockchain nodes increasing, the performance decreases sharply.

To solve the problems listed above, we may consider moving to the newest consensus algorithm - NoxBFT. In addition, we are working on using hardwares such as FPGA or GPU to achieve better performance.

Acknowledgment. This research was supported by the National Key R&D Program of China No. 2019YFB1404903.

References

1. Financial Stability Board: OTC Derivatives Market Reforms: 2019 Progress Report on Implementation, October 2019. https://www.fsb.org/
2. Bank for International Settlements: BIS Triennial Central Bank Survey of Foreign Exchange and Over-the-counter (OTC) Derivatives Markets, December 2019. https://www.bis.org
3. Li, S., et al.: The characteristics of smart contracts and their application in the bond market. ChinaBond Mag. **12**, 49–51 (2016)
4. Adamova, K.R., et al.: The digitalization of the russian financial market: the use of technologies of the distributed ledger by the institutions of Custodian infrastructure. J. Rev. Global Econ. 7, 497–509 (2018)
5. Lai, K.: DEAL: world's first global blockchain bond (bond-i). Int. Finan. Law Rev. (2018). www.iflr.com

6. Crabb, J.: Société Générale blockchain issuance a sign of things to come. Int. Financ. Law Rev. (2019). www.iflr.com
7. Ibrahim, A.: Does blockchain mean higher transparency in the financial sector? Revista de Comptabilitat i Direcció **27**, 69–81 (2018)
8. Spouse, T., et al.: How distributed ledger technology could solve regulatory problems. J. Financ. Compliance **3**, 60–66 (2019)
9. Kwon, O., et al.: Fintech, cryptoassets, and central bank digital currency in the Republic of Korea FutureOTC: an intelligent decentralized OTC Option Trading and E-contract Signing System. ADBI Working Paper Series (2019)
10. Bank of China: BOC issues special financial bonds of 20 billion yuan for small and micro enterprises (2019). www.bankofchina.com
11. Zhang, Q., Gao, J., Qin, Q., Wang, C., Yin, K.: FutureOTC: an intelligent decentralized OTC option trading and e-contract signing system. In: Si, X., et al. (eds.) CBCC 2019. CCIS, vol. 1176, pp. 17–30. Springer, Singapore (2020). https://doi.org/10.1007/978-981-15-3278-8_2
12. Leon, C., et al.: Practice and thinking of alliance blockchain. Commun. CCF **2**, 60–66 (2020)
13. People's Bank of China. (2020) Financial Distributed Ledger Technical Security Specification. wiki.hyperledger.org

A Group-Based Optimized Practical Byzantine Fault Tolerance Consensus Algorithm

Zhenshan Bao, Yue Liu, and Wenbo Zhang[✉]

Beijing University of Technology, 100 Pingleyuan, Chaoyang District, Beijing, China
{baozhenshan,zhangwenbo}@bjut.edu.cn, yuel@emails.bjut.edu.cn

Abstract. Focusing on the problems of high energy consumption, low efficiency and poor scalability of Practical Byzantine Fault Tolerance (PBFT) consensus algorithm existed in consortium blockchain, this paper presents a group-based optimized Practical Byzantine Fault Tolerance (GPBFT) consensus algorithm, which is a multi-stage algorithm. First, we propose a comprehensive reputation evaluation model to judge the credibility of a node from two aspects of transaction behavior and consensus performance. Then, the nodes with higher reputation value will be selected to enter the consensus group, and the other nodes with block packaging ability are selected as candidate nodes. Finally, we optimize the PBFT based on the application scenario of blockchain, change the three stages to two, which reduces the number of messages delivered by 50% at least. The experimental results demonstrate that GPBFT gains better performance. While ensuring the security and reliability of the system, it shows good scalability, thus it can be used in large-scale consortium blockchain system.

Keywords: Blockchain · Byzantine fault tolerance · Consensus · Reputation model · Multi-group

1 Introduction

Blockchain as the underlying technology of Bitcoin [1] is essentially a distributed ledger technology based on zero-trust foundation, decentralization and non-temperability, which are shared and maintained among distrustful nodes [2]. In short, it integrates technologies including distributed data storage technology, P2P network transmission mechanism, consensus mechanism between distributed nodes, encryption algorithms and programmable smart contracts, etc. Since "Bitcoin: A Peer-to-Peer Electronic Cash System" was proposed, blockchain has been paid more and more attention. Nowadays, the application scenarios of blockchain have been spread from cryptocurrency and digital asset to non-financial applications [3], such as property rights protection, credit system construction, education ecology optimization, food safety supervision, network security guarantee.

Generally, the type of blockchain deployment can be roughly divided into public blockchain, consortium blockchain and private blockchain. According to the different types of blockchain deployment, the existing consensus algorithms can be roughly

© Springer Nature Singapore Pte Ltd. 2021
K. Xu et al. (Eds.): CBCC 2020, CCIS 1305, pp. 95–115, 2021.
https://doi.org/10.1007/978-981-33-6478-3_7

divided into: Proof-of-X (PoX) consensus algorithms and Byzantine Fault Tolerant (BFT) consensus algorithms [4]. PoX is a new consensus protocol based on reward and punishment mechanism, such as PoW [1]. In order to meet the requirements of data throughput, resource utilization and security, improved protocols such as PoS [5] have been proposed, the basic feature of them is to design proof basis so that honest nodes can prove their legitimacy, thus realizing Byzantine fault tolerance. BFT refers to the traditional consensus protocol and its improved protocol [6], including PBFT [7], Zyzzyva [8], Tendermint [9], etc.

PBFT is a classical consistency algorithm based on state machine replication, which can reach a consensus when the number of Byzantine nodes is less than 1/3. It is widely used in consortium blockchain. With the gradual expansion of the scale of consortium blockchain application scenarios, although PBFT is a mature consensus algorithm, there are still some shortcomings. The first problem is the efficiency, in order to ensure the security in asynchronous mode, the three-stage broadcast process needs to consume the communication cost of polynomial level. Secondly, the primary node may be an invalid malicious node because of the random selection, it will lead to the occurrence of view changing, and then affect the efficiency. Finally, the scalability of the algorithm, the three-stage broadcast process requires the consent of $2/3n + 1$ nodes. In this process, replica nodes should broadcast messages to each other for Byzantine fault tolerance, the communication cost will increase polynomially as the number of nodes increases.

To counter the above problems, we propose a group-based optimized practical byzantine fault tolerance consensus algorithm (GPBFT), which narrow the number of consensus nodes down to a group of nodes with higher reputation values. On the one hand, the trustworthiness of nodes is evaluated comprehensively from two aspects of transaction behavior and consensus performance, so that the reputation evaluation of nodes is more accurate and reliable; on the other hand, GPBFT selects some nodes with the higher reputation to form a group to reach consensus, that will reduce the communication cost and resource consumption, the high scalability will more suitable for a large-scale network environment. Besides, we optimize the consensus algorithm based on PBFT, making the broadcast protocol changed from three stages to two. In this way, the transmission time is shortened, and the transmission rate is improved, thereby further improving the throughput and reducing the delay.

Overall, the main contributions of this paper are summarized as follows:

- We propose to use the reputation model to build a trusted consensus group with higher reputation value, which consists of two parts: transaction reputation and consensus reputation. It can prevent nodes with lower reputation values from participating in the consensus, reduce the number of nodes in the consensus process, and improve the efficiency.
- We divide the nodes with consensus ability into two groups: consensus group and candidate group. According to the change of the comprehensive reputation value, the nodes in the group are adjusted dynamically to ensure the high reliability of the nodes in the consensus group.

- We optimize the consensus algorithm based on PBFT, propose a new framework of GPBFT, make the broadcast protocol changed from three phases to two. According to the change of reputation value, the consensus nodes with low scores will be dynamically update, thus the members of consensus group are constantly changing.

The rest of this paper is organized as follows. Section 2 introduces background and related work, Sect. 3 describes system overview; Sect. 4 articulates the design process of GPBFT; Sect. 5 presents evaluation results; and Sect. 6 concludes this paper.

2 Background and Related Work

The Byzantine generals problem [6] is a basic problem that will be considered by consensus algorithm in blockchain. It is a protocol problem that describes the consistency of distributed systems. Byzantine fault tolerance can be expressed in the field of computers as: how to ensure the good operation of the system and the integrity, reliability and consistency of information data in the system network with malicious nodes, so as to make correct decisions.

Among the existing consensus algorithms, the classic distributed consensus algorithms [10] are Paxos [11], Raft [12] and PBFT. But, Paxos and Raft are data oriented rather than transaction oriented, the Byzantine issues were not taken into account, in other words, they don't consider the existence of malicious nodes in the system, once the malicious nodes send false messages, the whole system will store false error information.

In order to solve the Byzantine problem, PBFT is proposed. At present, the classification of BFT consensus algorithm can be divided into: state machine fault-tolerant algorithm, Byzantine fault-tolerant algorithm with trusted components and Byzantine fault-tolerant algorithm optimized for blockchain application scenarios.

The representative algorithms of state machine Byzantine system are PBFT and its improved algorithms, such as HQ (hybrid quorum) [13] replication which without master node sorting, Zyzzyva [8] which based on speculation, Zzyzx [14] which based on Byzantine locking, and Spining [15] optimized at the cost of master node handover, etc.

PBFT is introduced in detail below. The three-stage consensus flow of PBFT is shown in Fig. 1 [16], nodes are divided into primary node and replica nodes, four nodes are taken as examples, node C is the client, node0 is the primary node, node1, node2 and node3 are replica nodes, and node3 is a malicious node. When the client sends a request to the primary node, the algorithm begins to execute.

- First, after receiving the request, the primary node will assign a sequence number to the request and broadcast the pre-prepare message to all nodes.
- The replica nodes receiving the message verify the contents. If the verification is passed, the prepare message will be broadcasted to all other nodes.
- The nodes receiving the prepare messages verify the contents, and then broadcast the commit message to the all other nodes.
- The nodes receiving the commit messages will execute the request by the client and reply to it.

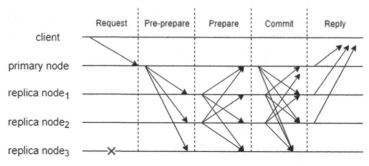

Fig. 1. PBFT normal operation

- The client waits for the same f + 1 replies and takes the replies as the execution result of the request.

There are also Byzantine fault-tolerant algorithms with trusted components and Byzantine fault-tolerant algorithm optimized for blockchain application scenarios. The representative algorithms of Byzantine system with trusted components are A2M [17], MinBFT [18], the main idea of the algorithms are using trusted hardwares to solve the problem of node identity uncertainty, so as to improve the Byzantine fault-tolerant ability and realize the ability improves to 2f + 1.

The algorithm optimized for blockchain application scenarios is Tendermint combined with POS and PBFT, the essence of the algorithm is PBFT. In addition, there is a kind of consensus algorithm based on cryptography, such as Algorand [19] with verifiable random number and HoneyBadgerBFT [20] using threshold signature to achieve asynchronous consensus. There is also an improved method to select a subset of network nodes as the committee, such as [21, 22] and [23], the algorithm will greatly enhance the centralization of blockchain by reducing the number of participating consensus nodes. Besides, the other BFT consensus algorithms such as RBFT [24], SBFT [25], CDBFT [26], and OuroborosBFT [27], are also proposed to improve PBFT. However, these algorithms are either with low efficiency or scalability.

3 System Overview

In our blockchain system, the operation of GPBFT is divided into a series of periods, and each period is divided into multiple slots. A block is generated in a slot, and a change of configuration information will update one period. Nodes update the reputation value once every slot, and dynamically adjust the members of consensus group once every period.

There are three types of nodes in the system: common nodes, consensus nodes, candidate nodes. The node identity and the relationship between nodes are shown in Fig. 2. Consensus group is composed of consensus nodes, and candidate group is composed of candidate nodes.

Common node: It does not have the ability to generate blocks, has no permission to participate in the block generation process, and can only join the block distribution

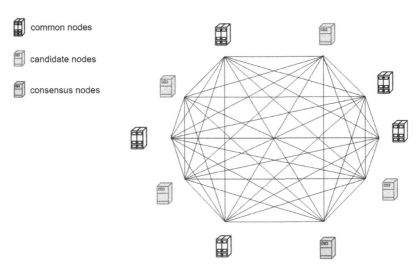

Fig. 2. Node identity and the relationship between nodes

and message forwarding process. They can see the whole consensus process and use the services of the system.

Consensus node: It has the ability to generate blocks and is responsible for generating blocks. It is the node that participates in the consensus process. They collect transaction information from the network, package them into a block, and then sign on it.

Candidate node: It has the ability to generate blocks, but doesn't participate in the block packaging work. It is used to eliminate the nodes at the bottom n of the consensus group.

The identity of consensus nodes and candidate nodes can be converted to the other, common nodes will not convert with other nodes because they don't have the ability to generate blocks.

Figure 3 show the overview of framework. GPBFT includes three stages: node trust evaluation, consensus group construction and consensus process. Firstly, the reputation model is introduced to calculate the comprehensive reputation value of nodes, which is the basis for selecting consensus group. Then, the nodes with higher reputation value are selected to form consensus group, which reduces the number of consensus nodes. After that, a new block will be connected to the blockchain. The performance of nodes in the consensus process will affect the consensus reputation value, and the comprehensive reputation value of nodes will be updated in time.

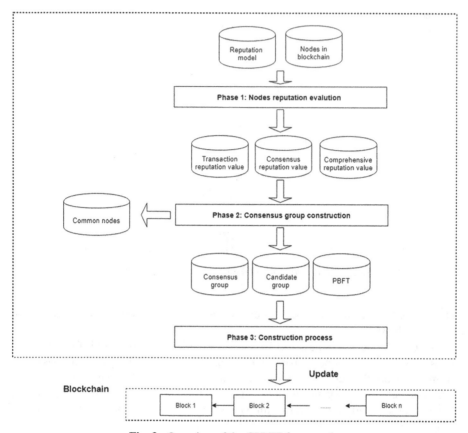

Fig. 3. Overview of the GPBFT framework

4 The Detail of GPBFT

4.1 Comprehensive Reputation Model

A credible consensus group with higher reputation value is constructed by comprehensive reputation model, which is composed of transaction and consensus reputation.

Transaction Reputation
According to the transaction history, the global transaction reputation value is calculated dynamically. The good and evil of the node can be judged, so as to reduce the probability that the malicious node is selected as the trading object or the member of the consensus group.

Definition

- Transaction: The interaction between two nodes in the distributed network, such as a business in the blockchain.

- Local transaction reputation (l_{ij}): The node evaluates the credibility of the node that has traded with it according to the transaction history. l_{ij} represents the reputation evaluation of node i to node j. The value range of l_{ij} is [0, 1], and the initial value is 0.5. The closer to 1, the more honest the node. When it's lower than 0.5, it's considered as a malicious node.
- Global transaction reputation (G_i): It is used to evaluate the transaction integrity of nodes from the perspective of the whole network. The value range and meaning of G_i are the same as that of l_{ij}

When the reputation value of malicious node is lower than the initial reputation value of 0.5, whitewashing attack may be caused: it will join the network as new node by changing their identity. The way to prevent this kind of attack is to strengthen the new user authentication management, and the consortium blockchain has strict identity audit and access mechanism, so whitewashing attack will not occur.

Local Transaction Reputation (l_{ij}) Evaluation Model

The node gives satisfaction or dissatisfaction evaluation after each transaction, and the local transaction reputation value is measured by the proportion of satisfaction times in the transaction record. Therefore, the calculation model of l_{ij} is as follow:

$$l_{ij} = \frac{N_h(i,j)}{N_h(i,j) + N_m(i,j) \times N_p} \tag{1}$$

In the formula (1), $N_h(i,j)$ and $N_m(i,j)$ denote the number of honest and malicious transactions between node i and j. It will be considered as malicious transactions that initiating a false transaction as a seller and failing to complete the transaction by appointment as a buyer in a transaction. N_p represents the punishment coefficient for malicious transactions, it makes the decline rate of reputation value faster than the rising.

Global Transaction Reputation (Gi) Evaluation Model

The global transaction reputation value calculation method is to take the average value of all the reputation evaluation values of the node.

$$G_i(k+1) = \frac{\sum_{j \in V_i} (G_j(k))^{N_w} \times \left(1 - e^{-\frac{N(j,i)}{5}}\right) \times l_{ji}}{\sum_{j \in V_i} (G_j(k))^{N_w} \times \left(1 - e^{-\frac{N(j,i)}{5}}\right)} \tag{2}$$

In the formula (2), $N(j,i) = N_h(j,i) + N_m(j,i)$, and it must be a positive integer, the initial global transaction reputation value $G_i(0) = 0.5$. N_w is the weighted coefficient of the evaluation node.

V_i is the set of nodes that have traded with node i, suppose $\{V_i\}$ represents the number of nodes in the set V_i, N_{min} is the minimum number of nodes participating in the evaluation of global value.

We construct a virtual node whose $G_v = 0.5$, $l_{ij} = 0.5$, $N(j,i) = +\infty$. If $\{V_i\} < N_{min}$, add $(N_{min} - \{V_i\})$ virtual nodes to complement, so that the number of nodes in the set V_i is not less than N_{min}. By specifying N_{min} in the evaluation, weakening the decisive role of a few nodes on a node evaluation, and can effectively prevent collective cheating. The value of N_{min} depends on the specific application.

The advantages of this weighted average method are:

The G_i of node i is jointly evaluated by the nodes that have traded with it;

The evaluation opinions of high trust nodes are more important than those of low;

The more transactions between nodes, the more credible the evaluation opinions between them;

The value is a process of gradual accumulation, and only the accumulation of continuous integrity transaction can obtain high reputation value;

The $k + 1$ round of the value calculation is based on the k round, without multiple iterations, reducing the communication and computing costs.

Consensus Reputation

The consensus reputation value is given to the node according to the behavior of participating in packing the block. In a period, only the nodes who enter the consensus group will change the value, and the initial value is 0.5. Suppose $\{S1, S2, S3...Sn\}$ represents the set of consensus nodes. The value will be dynamically granted by distinguishing honest or malicious signature behavior in each slot. We propose a dynamic measurement method based on logistic regression model, as shown in Formula 3:

$$C_i(cur) = \frac{1}{1 + e^{-\alpha\left(\sum_{x=0_x}^{n-1} \vartheta_x - \gamma \times \sum_{x=0_x}^{n-1} \tau_x\right)}} \tag{3}$$

$C_i(cur)$ is the consensus reputation value of node i given by the system according to the behavior before the current slot, n is the serial number of the current slot, α is the cumulative number of slots in a period that the node participates in, ϑ_x indicates whether node i normally replying in the x slot, If the node returns the correct information, $\vartheta = 1$,otherwise $\vartheta_x = 0$. τ_x indicates whether node i mistakenly replying in the x slot, if so, $\tau_x = 1$,otherwise $\tau_x = 0$. γ represents the penalty weight for malicious replying, which is set by the user.

In order to avoid the inaccurate judgment caused by the fast growth of reputation value in logistic regression model, this paper proposes a modified algorithm. According to the $C_i(cur)$ and the consensus reputation value at the beginning of the previous slot($C_i^{h-1}(t)$), the formula is:

$$\left(C_i^n(t) = \beta \times C_i(cur) + (1 - \beta) \times C_i^{n-1}(t)\right) \tag{4}$$

The consensus reputation of a node at the beginning of the first slot in the t period is equal to that at the end of the last slot of the $t-1$ period, $C_i^0(t) = C_i^{last}(t - 1)$, and $C_i^0(0) = 0.5$. The initial value of β is 1, because we don't know whether the node will have malicious tendency at first.

The change of β is based on the cumulative deviation $\xi_h^t C$, and the specific algorithm is determined as:

$$\beta = Td + m \times \frac{\delta_h^t C_i}{1 + \xi_h^t C} \tag{5}$$

Similarly, the cumulative deviation of reputation at the beginning of the t period is equal to that at the end of the last slot of the $t-1$ period, $\xi_0^t C = \xi_{last}^{t-1} C$ and $\xi_0^0 C = 0$. m is a user-defined parameter used to control the reaction weight to the node's recent behavior. Td is the threshold value which set to prevent β from supersaturation approaching 1, and its initial value is 0.25.

$\delta_h^t C$ represents the deviation of reputation, and its calculation method is shown in formula (6).

$$\delta_h^t C = \left| C_i^{n-1}(t) - C_i(cur) \right| \tag{6}$$

The node's deviation of reputation in consensus process at the n slot, is the absolute value of current reputation minus that the end of the last slot. The cumulative deviation is shown in formula (7).

$$\xi_h^t C = m \times \delta_h^t C + (1 - m) \times \xi_{h-1}^t C \tag{7}$$

A larger value of m given by the user indicates that the weight of the deviation is higher than the cumulative deviation.

In PBFT, when the client received the same $f + 1$ messages from $f + 1$ normal nodes, the consensus will be reached. According to formula (4), the value will not change for nodes that still have no reply when reaching a consensus. Obviously, it is unreasonable. So we design reputation consumption algorithm for these nodes:

$$C_i(cur) = \begin{cases} \dfrac{1}{1+e^{\alpha - \left(\sum_{x=0x}^{n-1} \partial x - \gamma \times \sum_{x=0x}^{n-1} \right)}}, & \text{when } \Delta B = 0 \\ C_i(cur) \times e^{-\Delta B}, & \text{In other case} \end{cases} \tag{8}$$

ΔB is the block interval, that is, the interval between the last block participated and the current block, if just two blocks are continuous, then $\Delta B = 0$, the consumption function will not be executed, which ensures that the nodes actively participate in the block verification online.

When the primary node changes, the consensus reputation value of it will be processed separately. As shown in formula (9).

$$C_i^0(t) = \begin{cases} 0.5, & \text{No packing} \\ C_i^{last}(t - 1) - 0.5, & \text{Packing a mistake block} \end{cases} \tag{9}$$

If the primary node doesn't pack the blocks on time, the consensus reputation value will drop to the initial value. If the packed block is mistake, the value will be directly subtracted by 0.5, which is lower than the initial value.

Comprehensive Reputation The node will be judged whether to enter the consensus group according to the ranking of the comprehensive reputation value. The calculation formula of it is as follows:

$$R_i = \varphi G_i + (1 - \varphi)C_i \tag{10}$$

Users can adjust the influence weight of transaction and consensus reputation value according to φ, and finally select nodes with higher value.

4.2 Construction of Consensus Group

In this section, we will introduce the process of constructing consensus group. We first initialize an empty consensus group, then sort all nodes according to their comprehensive reputation value, next exclude common nodes and the nodes whose transaction reputation value is less than 0.5. Given a constant percentage d of nodes and a $node_i$ in the set *Nodes*, if the value of $node_i$ is in the top percentage d, we add $node_i$ to consensus group, otherwise, it will be excluded.

Algorithm 1. getConsensus Group

```
Input: Node set Nodes, Comprehensive reputation value set
T, a constant d of nodes (0<d≤1)
Output: Consensus Group;Candidate Group
1    Consensus Group←∅;
2    Sort Nodes by T ;
3    for nodeᵢ ∈Nodes && consensus reputation value ≠ ∅ do
4      if transaction reputation value < 0.5 then
5          Exclude nodeᵢ from Consensus Group;
6      else if Ti is in the top d then
7          Add nodeᵢ into Consensus Group;
8          else
9          Add nodeᵢ into Candidate Group;
10            end
11      end
12    end
```

4.3 Consensus Process

The PBFT is based on the principle of state machine replication. The difficulty lies in how to ensure that all nodes perform the same sequence of operations. In order to ensure this, PBFT adopts three-stage protocol. But GPBFT is mainly designed for the blockchain, and the purpose is to reach a consensus on the transaction information of the whole network, it doesn't involve the ranking of requests. So the commit stage can be removed. Because the message has been broadcast in the whole network in the pre-prepare and prepare stages, all replica nodes have received the block information transmitted by the primary node, which only needs be verified.

Symbol Definition in Algorithm

The GPBFT includes two groups: consensus group and candidate group, which are represented by set R_1 and set R_2 respectively. The presentation of "promotion and demotion" rule can dynamically delete the nodes with low reputation value. If the maximum number of malicious nodes tolerated in the consensus group is f, then the set size must satisfy:

$$|R_1| \geq 3f + 1 \tag{11}$$

In general, $|R_1|$ is taken as $3f + 1$.

Nodes with top n reputation value in candidate group will replace the nodes in the consensus group whose value ranks at the bottom n. In general, the $|R_2|$, n should satisfy:

$$|R_2| \geq 2f, \; n = \frac{1}{2}f \tag{12}$$

- There is no client because of the change of C/S to P2P;
- The server information of consensus node is called configuration information, the nodes reach consensus in a same configuration information. The information's number is c and will increase in turn.
- The selection of primary node p is giving consideration to two things: the current block height h and configuration information's number c. Primary node is selected according to:

$$p = (h + c) \, mod \, |R_1| \tag{13}$$

- The replica nodes in the consensus group are represented by r and numbered by $\{0, 1, 2... |R_1|\}$, when the configuration information is changed, it should be numbered again.
- The consensus process can be divided into two stages: proposal and confirm.

The Flow of Algorithm

Without the initiator of the request, the primary node must initiate a consensus. We define the time interval for the primary node to initiate a consensus as Δ_t. When the primary node starts a consensus process, the transaction data and block information of honest consensus nodes are consistent. The consistency means that the configuration information number c, block height h, hash index of the previous block is same.

Based on the above contents, the detailed algorithm flow of GPBFT is as follows:

- When a transaction is initiated, the initiator signs the transaction with the private key and then broadcasts the transaction to the whole network.
- When a node receives the transaction, if it isn't a consensus node, the transaction will be relayed by flooding algorithm; if it is, the node needs to verify the legitimacy of the transaction. If the transaction is legal, it will be written to memory and recorded in the transaction field of the block data structure; if illegal, be discarded directly.
- After receiving the first transaction, each consensus node starts to construct the current block b according to c and the previous block information.
- After Δ_t, the node p sends the consensus proposal P_p to the replica nodes, and the message format is $\langle\langle Proposal, c, h, p, bd\rangle, block\rangle_{\sigma_p}$, $block$ is the block information and bd is a summary of $block$, $bd = Digest \, (block)$, adopting SHA-256 algorithm.
- After receiving the consensus proposal from primary node, the replica node r_i needs check whether the proposal is true, $i \in \{0, 1, 2...|R_1|-1\}$. If the proposal is true, a consensus confirmation message C_{s_i} will be sent to the other nodes. The message format is $< Confirm, c, h, ibd_{r_i} >_{\sigma_{r_i}}$, bd_{r_i} is the block summary information forwarded by r_i from node p.

- If the replica nodes check the proposal and find it isn't true, the nodes will suspect the primary node, then broadcast the configuration change message.
- When the node in the consensus group receives the other *2f* nodes' identical confirmation messages, it is considered that the consensus has been reached and can publish block from the primary node.
- After receiving the block, the rest of the nodes think that the consensus is completed, then they will delete the transactions contained in their memory and start a new round of consensus (Fig. 4).

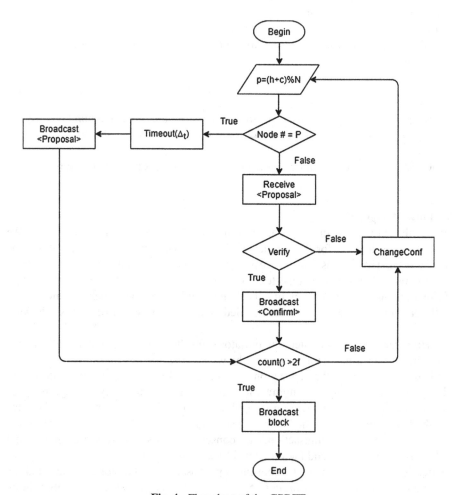

Fig. 4. Flowchart of the GPBFT

Transaction Confirmation

When the consensus nodes receive a transaction or the replica nodes check the transaction information in the block forwarded from the primary node, the rules for judging whether a transaction is legal are as follows:

- Whether the transaction complies with the written composition rules, if complies, it is legal.
- Whether the transaction has existed, if not, it is legal;
- Whether the transaction is double spending, the judgment of it is based on whether the previous block of the current is the last one. If it is, it's legal.
- Whether the script in the transaction is executed properly or not means that the property in the transaction is legally transferred from the initiator to the receiver. If it is executed correctly, it will be judged as legal.

In conclusion, the logic formula for judging the legitimacy of a transaction is:

$$IsValid\,(Transation) = (1)\&\&(2)\&\&(3)\&\&(4) \tag{14}$$

Configuration Change
If the replica node suspects the primary node or it didn't initiate a consensus proposal after the time of Δ_t when the process began, the replica node will initiate a configuration change message. The configuration change process is:

- The number of new configuration is c_{new}, $c_{new} = c_{old} + 1$, r' is the replica node sending the configuration change message, and the format is $< ChangeConf, c_{old}, c_{new}, r', h >_{\sigma_{s'}}$
- After receiving the message, other replica nodes reject the proposal and confirm message, but still listen and record the transaction data; then verify c_{old}, h whether consistent with themselves in the current configuration. If the information is same, $c_{new} = c_{old} + 1$, the node will broadcast the message as $< ChangeConfirm, c_{new}, c_{old}, h, i >_{\sigma_{r_i}}$.
- When the node in the consensus group receives the other $2f$ nodes' change confirm messages, the number of new configuration change to c_{new}.

5   Performance Evaluation

5.1   Algorithm Performance Analysis

Correctness
A correct blockchain system must satisfy two important characteristics of distributed system: safety and liveness. In consortium blockchain, they are defined as follows: safety means that all honest nodes will eventually submit consistent result, and liveness means that making the correct response to the transaction submitted by the client.

If a slave node is malicious, $2f + 1$ honest nodes would have reached a consistent result; if the primary node is a malicious node, which is the same as PBFT, GPBFT can provide liveness for the system by changing view.

When the view change occurs, $\frac{1}{2}f$ nodes with low reputation value in the consensus group will be replaced, and the number of malicious nodes in the consensus group will not exceed f. Through the continuous optimization of reputation model, consensus group will keep high reputation nodes to participate in consensus work. In summary, GPBFT can meet the requirements of security and activity.

Efficiency

In our algorithm, we reduce the amount of information delivered in the consensus process from two aspects: firstly, the consensus process is limited to the consensus group; secondly, we reduce the process into two stages.

We assume that there are n nodes in the current system, and select the nodes whose reputation value are the top d to participate in the consensus. When a consensus reached, the total communication times of PBFT are:

$$(dn - 1) + dn \times (dn - 1) = d^2n^2 - 1, \ 0 < d \le 1 \tag{15}$$

It is obvious that the number of messages delivered in the GPBFT will decrease significantly during the process of reaching an agreement. In practice, the system will directly define the nodes that don't possess consensus ability as common nodes when they register. Common nodes will not participate in the consensus process, so the actual number of nodes will be less than n.

Scalability

In the blockchain, most of the consensus algorithms based on Byzantine fault tolerance have poor scalability. When the number of nodes in the algorithm reaches a large scale, the performance will decline sharply. In GPBFT, through using a comprehensive trust model and constructing consensus groups, we reduce the number of nodes participating in the consensus process. It makes GPBFT more suitable for large-scale network environment.

5.2 Algorithm Performance Evaluation

Hyperledger Fabric is selected as the basic platform for the experiment. We improved Fabric v0.6 to implement the optimization algorithm. A prototype system is designed in Docker. The experimental environment is Intel i7-4702mq CPU 2.20 GHz and 16G RAM. Through the experimental model, we verify the change of nodes reputation value, and compare the delay and throughput with PBFT.

The Increase of Reputation Value

In the experiment, we set $n = 300$, $d = 0.1$. In transaction reputation model, $N_W = 1$, $N_p = 9$, $N_{min} = 30$. In consensus reputation model, $Td = 0.25$, $m = 0.5$.

As shown in Fig. 5, if a node always keeps honest trading and consensus behavior, its corresponding reputation value will continue to increase, but the growth is not infinite. The more honest the node is, the closer the value is to 1.

The Consumption of Reputation Value

Figure 6 shows the reputation value penalty in network nodes. In the transaction process,

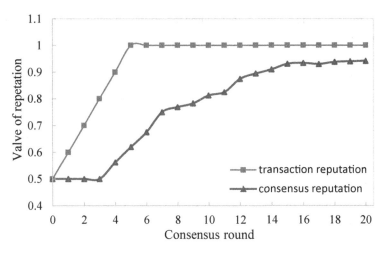

Fig. 5. Reputation value increase of node

if the node has malicious behavior, the transaction reputation value of the node will be reduced to less than 0.5 in a short period of time. At this time, it is recognized as a malicious node by the system, and then it has no chance to enter the consensus group.

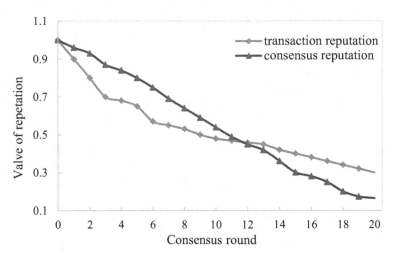

Fig. 6. Reputation value decline process

In Fig. 6, $node_i$ entered the consensus group successfully, and then in a period, it make 30% malicious behaviors in the consensus process. We set the penalty coefficient $\gamma = 0.3$. At the end of this period, the reputation value of $node_i$ is reduced to less than 0.5. When the consensus node is updated, it will be eliminated.

$Node_i$ entered the consensus group successfully, but when its consensus reputation value reaches the peak, it remains offline and no longer participates in the consensus process. At this time, the system will consume its reputation value, and the value decline process is shown in Fig. 7

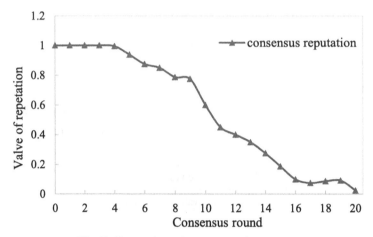

Fig. 7. Reputation value consumption process

It can be seen that if *node_i* doesn't participate in the consensus process, its reputation value can remain basically stable in the first few rounds, but from the fifth round, the value decreases significantly and presents a nonlinear decline process. It will decrease to below 0.5 in the 10th round, and gradually tend to 0 after the 17th round.

Transaction Throughput

In this experiment, we take $d = 0.3$, the values of time interval (the time of block generation) Δ_t are 10 s, 20 s, 60 s and 100 s respectively. Each time interval was tested 20 times, and the average of 20 times was taken as TPS. Figure 8 illustrates the number of transactions tested at different time intervals.

In order not to lose generality, the TPS value of GPBFT is taken as the average value of 120 times. That is, the relationship between TPS and the time of block generation is shown in Fig. 9. When the time interval is 20 s, the system performance reaches the peak, and then it will decline.

We also compare the throughput of PBFT and GPBFT in different time intervals, and the number of PBFT network nodes is 90. As shown in Fig. 9, the transaction throughput of GPBFT is much higher than PBFT. As time goes on, the throughput of PBFT remains basically unchanged. The GPBFT increases significantly in the early stage, the growth rate gradually slows down, finally tends to be stable. This is due to the good performance of the comprehensive reputation model. With the passage of time, the probability of Byzantine nodes participating in consensus gradually reduces, the

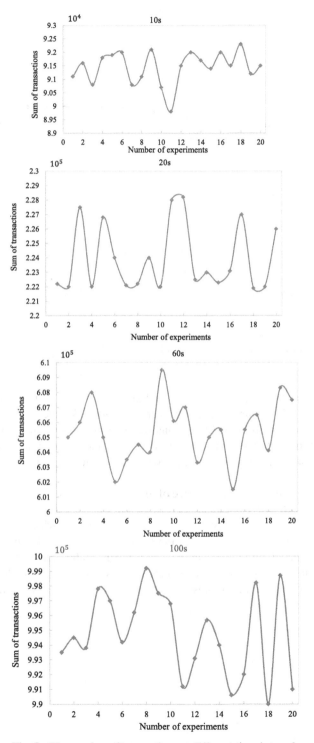

Fig. 8. The number of transactions at different time intervals

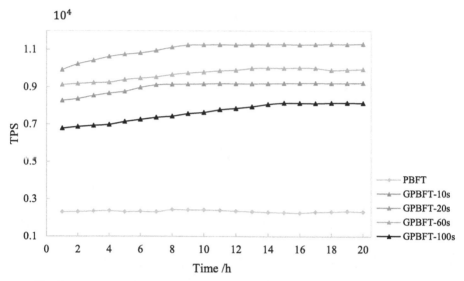

Fig. 9. Transaction throughput of PBFT and GPBFT in relation to number of nodes

frequency of view change significantly decreases. It means that the reputation model can effectively improve the reliability and stability of blockchain system.

Transaction Delay

Similarly, we take the values of time interval Δ_t are 10 s, 20 s, 40 s, 60 s, 100 s and 300 s respectively. We count 6 blocks in each case, and calculate the average value of all transaction delays within the block. Finally, we draw the graph of transaction delay under different time intervals as Fig. 10. It can be seen that the larger the value of Δ_t, the greater the transaction delay. When Δ_t, is within 60 s, the transaction delay has better performance.

In addition, we also test the influence of the different number of nodes on the delay, and compare it with PBFT, the details are shown in Fig. 11 ($\Delta_t = 20$). In general, the delay of PBFT increases rapidly with the increase of nodes, which is caused by the large number of messages delivered in the consensus process. Although the delay of GPBFT has similar situation, the overall delay is much smaller than PBFT. For different consensus group sizes, the smaller d is, the less message and the smaller delay. With the increase of d, the number of messages delivered will increase sharply, so the delay growth rate will increase.

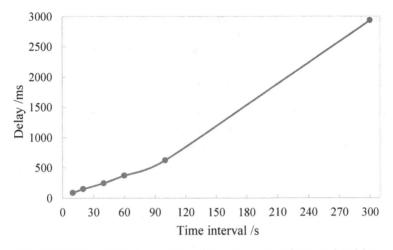

Fig. 10. Relationship between different time intervals and transaction delay

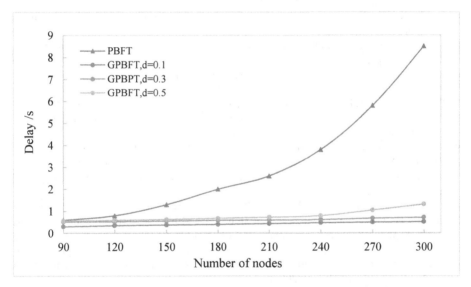

Fig. 11. Delay of PBFT and GPBFT in relation to number of nodes

6 Conclusion

In this paper, we propose a new consensus algorithm named GPBFT. A comprehensive reputation evaluation model introduced to judge the credibility of a node from two aspects of transaction behavior and consensus performance, choose the nodes with higher reputation to construct the consensus group, and select the other nodes with block packaging ability into candidate group. Besides, we optimize the PBFT consensus algorithm based on the application scenario to change the three stages to two, which reduces the communication cost significantly. GPBFT reduces the scale of consensus nodes through the establishment of consensus group, ensures the scalability of the system, reduces the delay by optimizing the consensus process, and makes the system more efficient. The use of reputation model can dynamically measure the credibility of nodes, and make the consensus process of the system always completed by nodes with higher reputation, which ensures the security and reliability. The experimental results show that GPBFT can dynamically remove nodes with low reputation values, there will be no centralization problem because of the establishment of the consensus group. With the continuous operation of the system, GPBFT has higher TPS and lower delay than PBFT, and is more suitable for large-scale consortium blockchain.

References

1. Nakamoto, S.: Bitcoin: A Peer-to-Peer Electronic Cash System. Manubot (2019)
2. Dinh, T.T.A., Liu, R., Zhang, M., et al.: Untangling blockchain: a data processing view of blockchain systems. IEEE Trans. Knowl. Data Eng. **30**(7), 1366–1385 (2018)
3. Khan, M.A., Salah, K.: IoT security: review, blockchain solutions, and open challenges. Future Gener. Comput. Syst. **82**, 395–411 (2018)
4. Yu, G., Zha, X., Wang, X., et al.: A unified analytical model for proof-of-x schemes. Comput. Secur. **96**, 101934 (2020)
5. King, S., Nadal, S.: PPCoin:peer-to-peer crypto-currency with proof-of-stake[J/OL]. (2017)https://peercoin.net/assets/paper/peercoin-paper.pdf
6. Lamport, L., Shostak, R., Pease, M.: The Byzantine generals problem. In: Concurrency: The Works of Leslie Lamport, pp. 203–226 (2019)
7. Castro, M., Liskov, B.: Practical byzantine fault tolerance. OSDI. **1999**(99), 173–186 (1999)
8. Kotla, R., Alvisi, L., Dahlin, M., et al.: Zyzzyva: speculative byzantine fault tolerance. ACM Trans. Comput. Syst. (TOCS) **27**(4), 1–39 (2010)
9. Kwon, J.: Tendermint: consensus without mining. Draft v. 0.6, fall, **1**(11) (2014)
10. Zheng, Z., Xie, S., Dai, H., et al.: An overview of blockchain technology: architecture, consensus, and future trends. In: 2017 IEEE International Congress on Big Data (BigData congress), pp. 557–564. IEEE (2017)
11. Lamport, L.: Paxos made simple. ACM SIGACT News **32**(4), 18–25 (2001)
12. Ongaro, D., Ousterhout, J.: In search of an understandable consensus algorithm. In: 2014 USENIX Annual Technical Conference ({USENIX}{ATC} 14), 305–319 (2014)
13. Cowling, J., Myers, D., Liskov, B., et al.: HQ replication: a hybrid quorum protocol for Byzantine fault tolerance. In: Proceedings of the 7th Symposium on Operating Systems Design and Implementation, 177–190 (2006)
14. Hendricks, J., Sinnamohideen, S., Ganger, G.R., Reiter, M.K.: Zzyzx: scalable fault tolerance through Byzantine locking. In: 2010 IEEE/IFIP International Conference on Dependable Systems & Networks (DSN). IEEE, pp. 363–372 (2010)
15. Veronese, G.S., Correia, M., Bessani, A.N., Lung, L.C.: Spin one's wheels? Byzantine fault tolerance with a spinning primary. In: 28th IEEE International Symposium on Reliable Distributed Systems, pp. 135–144. IEEE (2009)
16. Castro, M., Liskov, B.: Practical Byzantine fault tolerance and proactive recovery. ACM Trans. Comput. Syst.(TOCS) **20**(4), 398–461 (2002)
17. Chun, B.G., Maniatis, P., Shenker, S., Kubiatowicz, J.: Attested append-only memory: making adversaries stick to their word. ACM SIGOPS Oper. Syst. Rev. **41**(6), 189–204 (2007)
18. Veronese, G.S., Correia, M., Bessani, A.N., Lung, L.C., Verissimo, P.: Efficient byzantine fault-tolerance. IEEE Trans. Comput. **62**(1), 16–30 (2011)

19. Gilad, Y., Hemo, R., Micali, S., Vlachos, G., Zeldovich, N.: Scaling byzantine agreements for cryptocurrencies. In: Proceedings of the 26th Symposium on Operating Systems Principles, pp. 51–68 (2017)
20. Miller, A., Xia, Y., Croman, K., Shi, E., Song, D.: The honey badger of BFT protocols. In: Proceedings of the 2016 ACM SIGSAC Conference on Computer and Communications Security, pp. 31–42 (2016)
21. Heo, H.S., Seo, D.Y.: A study on scalable PBFT consensus algorithm based on blockchain cluster. J. Inst. Internet, Broadcast. Commun. **20**(2), 45–53 (2020)
22. Jalalzai, M.M., Busch, C., Richard, G.G.: Proteus: a scalable BFT consensus protocol for blockchains. In; 2019 IEEE International Conference on Blockchain (Blockchain), pp. 308–313. IEEE (2019)
23. Meng, Y., Cao, Z., Qu, D.A.: Committee-based byzantine consensus protocol for blockchain. In: IEEE 9th International Conference on Software Engineering and Service Science (ICSESS), pp. 1–6. IEEE (2018)
24. Lei, K., Zhang, Q., Xu, L., et al.: Reputation-based byzantine fault-tolerance for consortium blockchain. 2018 In: IEEE 24th International Conference on Parallel and Distributed Systems (ICPADS), pp. 604–611. IEEE (2018)
25. Gueta, G.G., Abraham, I., Grossman, S., et al.: SBFT: a scalable decentralized trust infrastructure for blockchains. arXiv preprint arXiv:1804.01626 (2018)
26. Wang, Y., Cai, S., Lin, C., Chen, Z., Wang, T., Gao, Z., Zhou, C.: Study of blockchains's consensus mechanism based on credit. IEEE Access **7**, 10224–10231 (2019)
27. Kiayias, A., Russell, A.: Ouroboros-BFT: a simple byzantine fault tolerant consensus protocol. IACR Cryptol. ePrint Arch. **2018**, 1049 (2018)

Storage Optimization for Certificates in Blockchain Based PKI System

Junzhi Yan[✉], Bo Yang, Li Su, and Shen He

China Mobile Research Institute, Beijing, China
{yanjunzhi,yangbo,suli,heshen}@chinamobile.com

Abstract. In recent years, many researches on decentralized PKI (Public Key Infrastructure) by using block technology have emerged to prevent problems faced by tradition PKI, such as single point of failure. Certificates are recorded into the decentralized blockchain in many of the researches. With the increased number of certificates, the blockchain based PKI system will occupy a considerable amount of storage space. In this paper, the framework of blockchain based PKI system is introduced, and optimizations for certificate storage are provided. The certificates have expiry dates, and the optimization based on the invalid certificates is proposed. In many applications and scenarios, the target certificates are explicit, and then the optimization based on the target certificates is proposed. These optimization methods could improve the storage efficiency of specific nodes in blockchain based PKI system.

Keywords: Blockchain · PKI · Storage optimization

1 Background

PKI (Public Key Infrastructure) has been widely used in the Internet to support identification/authentication, integrity and confidentiality. CA (Certification Authority) is the trust anchor of PKI system. The centralized CA infrastructure has become one of the most vulnerable and valuable attack targets. There was once some CA that went bankrupt because of malicious security attacks [1, 2]. The unavailability of centralized CRL/OCSP (Certificate Revocation List/Online Certificate Status Protocol) service will affect the service system, and it will make the service not be as secure as expected. Blockchain is decentralized, and all the nodes collaborate to record the transactions into the ledger and maintain a consistency of the ledger. The compromise of a node will not tamper the transactions in the ledger. Besides, even some nodes do not work, the distributed and redundancy storage could help to protect the availability and consistent of the ledger. These features may help to prevent the single point of failure in PKI system. Many blockchain based researches about decentralized PKI have been emerged to solve such attacks.

Usually, blockchain contains all the historical transactions. With the increased number of certificates, the blockchain based PKI system will occupy a considerable amount of storage space. The certificate inquiry efficiency will be decreased with the increased

K. Xu et al. (Eds.): CBCC 2020, CCIS 1305, pp. 116–125, 2021.
https://doi.org/10.1007/978-981-33-6478-3_8

number of certificates in the system. Some methods to optimize the storage expense and to enhance the computation efficiency were proposed in [3–5]. These researches focus on the universal blockchain storage, while in this paper the optimization related with certificate characteristics will be considered.

Section 2 shows the related works about blockchain based PKI. The framework of blockchain based PKI is given in Sect. 3. The invalid certificate storage optimization and target certificate optimization are provided in Sect. 4. Section 5 provides security analysis and limitations. The conclusion is in Sect. 6.

2 Related Works on Blockchain Based PKI

DPKI is a set of requirements on how to implement identity management in a decentralized manner [6]. The basic idea is to give full control over an identifier to its owner.

The implementation of Yakubov et al. [7] uses the standard X.509v3 certificate with an addition to the extension fields to indicate its location in the blockchain. The smart contract of each CA contains one list with all issued certificates and another list for revoked certificates.

BlockPKI [8] requires multiple CAs to perform a complete domain validation from different vantage points for an increased resilience to compromise and hijacking, scale to a high number of CAs by using an efficient multi-signature scheme, and provide a framework for paying multiple CAs automatically.

CertLedger [9] is a PKI architecture with certificate transparency based on blockchain to eliminate the split-world attacks and to provide certificate/revocation transparency.

Namecoin [10] is a Bitcoin fork which is designed to act as a decentralized DNS for ".bit" addresses.

Certcoin [11] is based on Namecoin, and use blockchain to record the domain names and public keys, so as to implement server authentication in certcoin system.

EmerSSL [12] proposed a method to provide SSL certificates service to launch client authentication. The client generates a certificate and publishes to EmerSSL. Then the client can authenticate itself during SSL connection.

SCPKI [13] works on Ethereum blockchain, and uses an entity or authority in the system to verify another entity's identity. It could be used to detect rogue certificates when they are published.

Research in [14] focuses on the trust among multiple CAs using blockchain, and provides some use cases in mobile networks. Research on blockchain based logs could be found in [15].

Standard development organizations such as ISO/IEC, ITU-T have begun to study and standardize blockchain based PKI and certificate management technology.

Blockchain based PKI has become a significant direction for PKI technology. All the above researches focus on the structure and usage of blockchain to facilitate PKI and certificate management, but have not discussed the storage of certificates. With the increase of blockchain ledger, the storage space for certificates needs to be considered. The main contribution of this paper focuses on the optimization, which will slow down the speed of the increased certificate storage space.

3 Framework of Blockchain Based PKI

A blockchain system contains mounts of independent nodes. All the nodes autonomously generate and distribute legitimate transactions into the blockchain system, and collaborate to record the transactions into the ledger and maintain a consistency of the ledger. The ledger is available and replicated across the nodes in the system. Each node in the system could have its own copy of all the blocks. Even some nodes do not work, or have been compromised, the storage redundancy help to protect the availability and consistent of the ledger. The compromise of a node will not tamper the transactions in the ledger. These features of blockchain may help to prevent the single point of failure in PKI system.

Figure 1 shows the framework of blockchain based PKI system. There are several stakeholders in the framework of blockchain based PKI system, i.e., certificate users, relying parties, validator nodes, inquiry nodes.

– Certificate user is the owner of the certificate. It could be a device or software client in mobile networks.
– Relying party is an entity that relies on the data in a public key certificate in making decisions [16]. The relying party is responsible to check the validity of the certificate by checking the certificate status.
– Validator node is the node to verify the received requests and generate new ledgers. The submitted certificates will be verified, only the verified certificates could be recorded into the ledger. They could be held by vendors, operators and service providers, and they could also be held by CAs.
– The inquiry node provides certificate inquiry services. The service includes the certificate inquiry and certificate status inquiry.

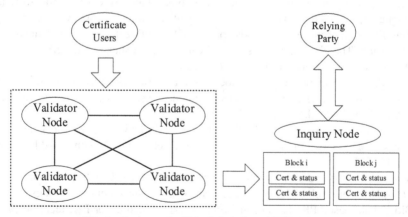

Fig. 1. Framework of blockchain based PKI system

Certificate user generates a self-signed certificate and submits it to the blockchain based PKI system. The validator nodes will verify the submitted certificates. The validation contains the identity information of the certificate user, and the profile of the certificates. For example, the ownership of the domain name in SSL certificates, while the device identity in device certificates needs to be verified. The verification policies could be customized according to certificate types and scenarios. New certificates with the status "normal" will be recorded into the ledger after validation and consensus.

The trustworthy of certificates relies on whether they are recorded in the ledger of the blockchain. Any entity with the capability to access the blockchain based PKI system could provide certificate and certificate status inquiry service. The traditional centralized CRL/OCSP service [17] could be replaced by the decentralized certificate status inquiry service, and then the single point of failure of CRL/OCSP service could be avoided.

In 5G network, SBA (Service-based Architecture) domain security is a significant security feature [18]. TLS (Transport Layer Security) will be used to secure the communication between network functions. Traditionally, the TLS certificates are issued by the commonly used commercial CA, so as to ensure the certificates could be verified by the client. However, the devices are deployed in the operator's core network with no connection to the Internet, which means both CRL and OCSP services are unavailable. The system will not be as secure as expected.

By using blockchain based solution, a TLS server generates a self-signed certificate, which contains the server's domain name. The certificate is submitted into the blockchain based PKI system. The validator nodes verify the certificate. The verification includes the profile, the domain name's ownership, etc. After the verification, the certificate will be recorded into the ledger. An edge entity, which is deployed on the edge of intranet and Internet, could be launched as an inquiry node to provide certificate inquiry service for the intranet.

4 Certificate Storage Optimization in Blockchain Based PKI System

4.1 Optimization for Invalid Certificates

The certificate has an expiration date. If the certificate expires, or it is revoked, the certificate is invalid and will be no longer trusted. Due to this characteristic, the storage space could be optimized.

When all the certificates in a block are invalid, the body of the block can be deleted from the blockchain. The block header remains to ensure the integrity of the ledger. This optimization method applies to the inquiry nodes in Fig. 1.

The nodes in blockchain based PKI system may record the complete certificate, while in some cases it records the hash of certificates. The optimization process is a little different. If a node records complete certificates, the optimization could be done by the node itself. Otherwise, if the node records certificate hashes, the optimization should be done by the help of a special node, which maintains all the complete certificates. It could be called as a full node.

The full node checks the certificates in each block. If all certificates in some block are invalid, the full node would send a message containing the block identifier to the nodes which contains certificate hashes. This message also contains all the certificates in the block which will be optimized.

The node containing certificate hashes verifies the certificates in the above message and their hashes in the ledger. Then it checks the expiration date and the status. If the certificates are all invalid, the inquiry node deletes the body of the block.

4.2 Optimization for Target Certificates

In practice, the users in some service systems are explicit to the system. For example, the security gateway of a service system can be used to authenticate devices or users using PKI technology, such as the H(e)NB (Home NodeB or Home eNodeB) scenario specified in [19]. Only the registered devices and users could be authenticated by the security gateway. In such scenarios, the devices and users provide certificates to the security gateway, which uses the certificates to authenticate the devices and users. The security gateway only needs some of the certificates recorded in the ledger, but not all of them. The authenticated devices and users are the certificate users, while the security gateway is the relying party in Fig. 1. The security gateway could consist of the function of inquiry node to achieve local certificate inquiry, which is a lightweight node in the blockchain system. It only needs to receive new blocks, but not need to participate into the generation of new blocks. If the security gateway keeps the necessary blocks, it could authenticate the devices and users locally, by using the certificate.

These certificates are recorded in the scattered blocks. If some block does not contain any of the certificates used by the security gateway, the block is unnecessary to be kept by the security gateway. However, the security gateway has to keep these blocks to ensure the integrity of the blockchain ledger. An optimization for the unnecessary blocks could be launched.

In such scenario, the security gateway only needs to keep the blocks containing necessary certificates. Since the necessary certificates are scattered in the non-consecutive blocks. Concatenation nodes are used to connect these non-consecutive blocks. The security gateway will keep the non-consecutive blocks, and some concatenation blocks. A concatenation block contains the following information:

- Previous pointer: to record the previous block header's hash of the first block in the consecutive deleted blocks.
- Next pointer: to record the subsequent block header's hash of the last block in the consecutive deleted blocks.
- Checksum: the hash of all the headers from the first block to the last block in the consecutive deleted blocks.

The previous pointer points to the previous block of the deleted consecutive blocks, and the next pointer points to the next block of the deleted blocks. The hash of previous header in the block which is pointed by the next pointer points to the last block of the deleted blocks. These information is used to verify the concatenation block.

Figure 2 shows the traditional blockchain blocks. If some node, such as the security gateway, does not need to use the certificates recorded in the ledgers from block i to block j, the node could delete the blocks from block i to block j, as the following method.

Denote the hash value of the header in block k as h_k, the node is required to calculate the following parameters, if the blocks from block i to block j needs to be deleted:

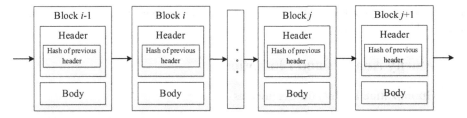

Fig. 2. Blockchain blocks

- Previous pointer: h_{i-1}.
- Next pointer: h_{j+1}.
- Checksum: merkle root of $h_i, h_{i+1}, ..., h_{j-1}, h_j$.

Then the node could delete block i, block j, and all the blocks between them. By using the above parameters, a concatenation block is used to connect block $i-1$ to block $j+1$, as shown in Fig. 3. In the concatenation block p, the previous pointer is the header's hash of block $i-1$, the next pointer is the header's hash of block $j+1$, while the checksum is the merkle root of $h_i, h_{i+1}, ..., h_j$. The next pointer points to block $j+1$, while the hash of previous header in block $j+1$ points to block j.

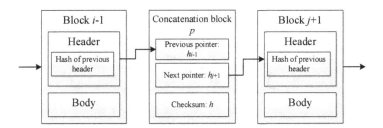

Fig. 3. Optimized blocks of blockchain

Based on the optimization in Fig. 3, it could be optimized continuously if the block pointed by the next pointer (block $j+1$) could be deleted. The next pointer in the concatenation block is the hash value of the header in block $j+2$, the previous pointer is the hash of the previous header (h_{i-1}). The checksum is the merkle root of $hi, ..., h_j$, h_{j+1}. The hash of the header in block $j+1$ works as a new leaf in the merkle tree.

Based on the optimization in Fig. 3, if the block pointed by the previous pointer (block $i-1$) could be deleted, the merkle tree needs to be reconstructed. The reconstruction needs the hashes of the headers from block $i-1$ to block $j+1$. The optimized node needs to inquire these headers' information. It shows the forward scalability of the optimization mechanism is better than backward scalability.

By using the above method, the optimized node does not need to keep all the blocks in the blockchain based PKI system, but only needs to store the blocks containing the certificates needed by the service. Since these blocks are not consecutive, the node uses concatenation blocks to ensure the non-consecutive blocks keep the chain structure. With the generation of new blocks, the optimized node could receive new blocks, and record the new blocks containing the certificates it requires.

5   Security Analysis and Limitations

5.1   Optimization for Invalid Certificates

The optimization method for invalid certificates deletes the block bodies in which all certificates are invalid. It does not change the structure of the blocks. The integrity of each block could be guaranteed by the block header, and then the integrity of the ledger could also be guaranteed. The essence of this optimization method is the SPV (Simplified Payment Verification) of bitcoin [20]. It relies on the security of the blockchain based PKI system.

This optimization applies to the inquiry nodes, but not the nodes used for validation or generation of new blocks. However, if there is a need for certificates backup, the optimization works in the inquiry node, while another node is necessary to store all the blocks and all the certificates.

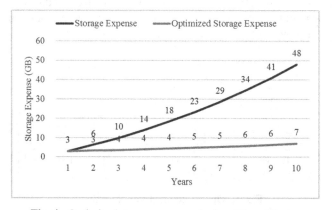

Fig. 4. Optimized storage expense for invalid certificates

Assuming that 10 million certificates are recorded in the blockchain based PKI system, and the number increases 10% per year. It is assumed that the average validity of the certificates is 2-years long, each certificate occupies 300 bytes. Figure 4 shows the storage expense of blockchain based PKI system, if the optimization method for invalid certificates is adopted. It shows the storage expense increases a little after optimization, while it increases linearly without optimization. In the next 10 years, the optimized storage expense will arise to 7 GB, while it will arise to 48 GB without optimization. About 85% storage space will be saved if it is optimized.

5.2   Optimization for Target Certificates

Assuming that 10 million certificates are recorded in the blockchain based PKI system, and there are 200,000 target certificate users which will connect the security gateway in the mobile network. A storage space of more than 3 GB is required to keep all the certificates. In our simulation, each block contains 100 certificates on average, and the 200,000 target certificates are scatted in 20,000 blockchain blocks. By using the optimization for target certificates, 2000 blockchain blocks and 2000 concatenate blocks are required. Each concatenate block occupies 100 Bytes. As a result, a storage of 60 MB is required for the security gateway, as shown in Fig. 5.

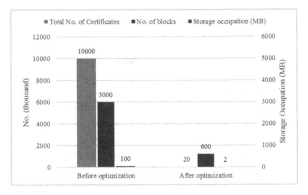

Fig. 5. Optimized storage expense for target certificates

The optimization for the target certificates changes the original structure of the blocks, so some attacks may happen.

1. Fake pointer attack

If a node in the blockchain based PKI system uses a concatenate block to connect two non-consecutive blocks. Attackers could compromise the optimized node, tamper with the next pointer in the concatenate block, and make it point to a fake block. As shown in Fig. 6, the next pointer points to block $j' + 1$, which is a fake block.

To avoid this attack, the node needs to verify the checksum in the concatenate block, to ensure the concatenate block contain the correct information of blocks which have been deleted. Then it also needs to verify and ensure the hash of previous header in the block (block $j + 1$) pointed by the next pointer is the same as the header hash of block j. For example, the hash of previous header in block $j' + 1$ should be the same as the header hash of block j'.

2. Fake concatenation block attack

Some optimized node in the blockchain based PKI system may launch attacks to other nodes. It uses a concatenate block to connect two non-consecutive blocks, and then it generates a fake concatenation block and send this block to other nodes. If some node receives this fake information without validation, the fault blocks pointed by the fake concatenation block could be introduced into the system.

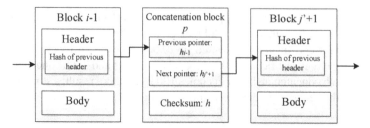

Fig. 6. Fake pointer attack

To avoid this attack, each node needs to generate the concatenation block by itself. If the node gets concatenation information from other nodes, it needs to verify the information before acceptance.

The node in each service system could use optimization for the target certificates, and delete blocks if necessary. Actually, nodes in different service systems need different certificates, and then the optimization results are different. This method applies to the local optimization of the service system, but not applies to the validator nodes which are used for validation and generation of new blocks.

5.3 Constraints and Limitations

The above optimizations apply to the inquiry nodes working for the specific application service and for local certificates inquiry, but not the nodes participating into the endorsement of new transactions and the generation of new blocks.

6 Conclusion

Decentralized PKI is a significant trend for PKI technology. The framework of blockchain based PKI system is introduced in this paper, it can be used to solve some problems faced by traditional PKI technology. Optimizations for the certificate storage are provided. The optimization method based on the invalid certificates is proposed, since certificates have expiry dates. In many applications and scenarios, the targeted certificates are explicit, and then the optimization method based on the targeted certificates is proposed. These optimization methods can be used simultaneously and improve the storage efficiency in blockchain based PKI system. Storage optimization can be launched in inquiry nodes to enhance the storage and computation efficiency. This work could also facilitate the certificate usage in 5G networks.

References

1. Nicole, M.: DigiNotar: dissecting the first dutch digital disaster. J. Strateg. Secur. **6**(2), 46–58 (2013)
2. Hepp, T., Spaeh, F., Schoenhals, A., et al.: Exploring potentials and challenges of blockchain-based public key infrastructures. In: IEEE INFOCOM 2019: IEEE Conference on Computer Communications Workshops, pp. 847–852 (2019)

3. Back, A., Corallo, M., Dashjr, L.: Enabling Blockchain Innovations with Pegged Sidechains (2014). https://www.opensciencereview.com/papers/123/enablingblockchain-inn ovations-with-pegged-sidechains

4. Gao, J., Li, Bo., Li, Z.: Blockchain storage analysis and optimization of bitcoin miner node. In: Liang, Q., Liu, X., Na, Z., Wang, W., Mu, J., Zhang, B. (eds.) CSPS 2018. LNEE, vol. 517, pp. 922–932. Springer, Singapore (2020). https://doi.org/10.1007/978-981-13-6508-9_112

5. Wei, X., Chen, J., Li, Z.: Research on optimization model of storage capacity based on the consortium blockchain. In: Liang, Q., Liu, X., Na, Z., Wang, W., Mu, J., Zhang, B. (eds.) CSPS 2018. LNEE, vol. 517, pp. 911–921. Springer, Singapore (2020). https://doi.org/10. 1007/978-981-13-6508-9_111

6. Allen, C., Brock, A., Vitalik, B., et al.: Decentralized Public Key Infrastructure (2015). https:// www.weboftrust.info/downloads/dpki.pdf

7. Yakubov, A., Shbair, W.M., Wallbom, A., et al.: A blockchain-based PKI management framework. In: NOMS 2018: 2018 IEEE/IFIP Network Operations and Management Symposium, Taipei, pp. 1–6 (2018)

8. Dykcik, L., Chuat, L., Szalachowski, P., et al.: BlockPKI: an automated, resilient, and transparent public-key infrastructure. In: 2018 IEEE International Conference on Data Mining Workshops (ICDMW), Singapore, pp. 105–114 (2018)

9. Kubilay, M., Kiraz, M., Mantar, H.: CertLedger: a new PKI model with certificate transparency based on blockchain. Comput. Secur. **85**, 333–352 (2019)

10. Namecoin. https://www.namecoin.org/

11. Fromknecht, C., Velicanu, D., Yakoubov, S.: Certcoin: A namecoin based decentralized authentication system. Massachusetts Inst. Technol., Cambridge, MA, USA, Technical Report, vol. 6 (2014)

12. EMCSSL. Decentralized identity management, passwordless logins, and client SSL certificates using Emercoin NVS (2015). https://emercoin.com/zh/emerssl

13. An, H., Kim, K.: QChain: quantum-resistant and decentralized PKI using blockchain. In: 2018 Symposium on Cryptography and Information Security (SCIS 2018) (2018)

14. Yan, J., Peng, J., Zuo, M., et al.: Blockchain based PKI certificate system. Telecom Engineering Technics and Standardization, pp. 16–20 (2017)

15. Lewison, K., Corella, F.: Backing rich credentials with a blockchain PKI (2016)

16. ITU-T X.509. The Directory: Public-key and attribute certificate frameworks (2016)

17. IETF RFC 5280. Internet X.509 Public Key Infrastructure Certificate and Certificate Revocation List (CRL) Profile (2008)

18. 3GPP TS 33.510, Security architecture and procedures for 5G system (2019)

19. 3GPP TS 33.320, Security of Home Node B (HNB)/Home evolved Node B (HeNB) (2018)

20. Nakamoto, S.: Bitcoin: A peer-to-peer electronic cash system (2008). https://www.bitcoin. org/en/bitcoin-paper

Author Index

Printed in the United States
By Bookmasters